HOBBES
AND HIS CRITICS

HOBBES
AND HIS CRITICS

A Study in
Seventeenth Century Constitutionalism

JOHN BOWLE

'*For the English always desired to be governed as men, not as Asses . . . This is the quality of all understanding people of other nations.*'

The Reverend George Lawson *An Examination of the Political Part of Mr. Hobbs his Leviathan, 1657.*

FRANK CASS & CO. LTD
1969

This edition published by

FRANK CASS AND COMPANY LIMITED

67 Great Russell Street, London WC1

First published by Jonathan Cape

First edition	1951
New impression with corrections	1969

SBN 7146 1548 X

Printed in Great Britain by
Clarke, Doble & Brendon Ltd., London and Plymouth

CONTENTS

To
Sir Maurice Bowra,
Warden of Wadham;
eminent successor
of
Dr. John Wilkins

PREFACE

As the pioneer of a utilitarian concept of government based upon a philosophy of radical scepticism, Hobbes is universally accorded a prominent place in the history of political thought. His fame is not merely academic: he is well known among all who are interested in political ideas. While the names of his opponents are forgotten, he still retains a prestige which would gratify though it would not surprise him.

Yet in spite of the considerable volume of Hobbesian studies, no systematic account has hitherto been taken of the political criticisms his work evoked from his contemporaries. Clarendon's attack on him is fairly well known, if little read, the Reverend George Lawson's abilities as a forerunner of John Locke are beginning to be recognized, and the spirited onslaughts of Bishop Seth Ward and of Bishop Bramhall are familiar to students of the mid-seventeenth century; but Dr. Eachard's knock-about dialogues and the indictment of the able barrister, John Whitehall, have fallen into undeserved neglect. This obscurity is shared by the pamphlet of Dr. Lucy, that rather dim Bishop of St. David's, and by the work of the academic virtuoso, Alexander Rosse, whose memory survives mainly through a Byronic rhyme in *Hudibras*. These writers, with their striking metaphors and epigrammatic style, also provide a cross section of contemporary opinion. Some of them contributed directly to the development of the Whig political tradition of which Locke was to become the most famous exponent, and which was to exercise so deep an influence upon English and American political thought and institutions. In this context, along with an account of Lawson, some description of the ideas of Philip Hunton, another forerunner of Locke, has also been included.

Hobbes stands today as a contributor to an outlook which dominated nineteenth-century English political thought through the writings of Bentham and his followers, and through Austin's definition of positive law; the novelty of his approach is apparent from the opposition he provoked among his contemporaries. His view of the State was fundamentally different from the old tradition of constitutional commonwealth, and for a full understanding of the *Leviathan*, an appreciation of Hobbes' impact on his contemporaries is indispensable. Their criticism emphasizes Hobbes' originality, making him stand out against his background.

But how far were these critics effective? Do they succeed in answering Hobbes? How far is a modern estimate of him modified by taking them into account? Or have they no more significance than the chatter of sparrows mobbing a hawk?

Their own age thought them formidable; so did the eighteenth century. All these writers believed in a divine and transcendental sanction for society. To them government was not a mere convenience, but the expression of a cosmic order. Hobbes was attempting to design a state independent of these sanctions. Whether this attempt is necessary, and whether it is practicable, is a question not yet decided. Even if the traditional view has to be abandoned, it is unlikely that any society can be successful without some belief more inspiring than a bleak utilitarianism. By their eloquence these critics call attention to the profound implications of Hobbes' challenge, and by their unanimity, to the deep psychological need for a social *mystique*. They emphasize the inadequacy of a purely rationalistic social programme, the importance of the distinction between society and government, and the need to maintain a standard whereby state power can be judged.

On the immediate political level their contribution is also valuable. These writers were representative of seventeenth-century England. They were forerunners of Locke, with his world influence on the practice of constitutional government. They represented a tradition which had come down from antiquity and the Middle Ages, and which was to inspire the political organization of vast areas of the world. To them Hobbes seemed an unstatesmanlike writer. And original as was his insight, trenchant his genius as a political philosopher, it cannot be said that Hobbes was a practical politician. It was Whig constitutionalism and not Hobbes' authoritarian state which determined the development of eighteenth-century England, with all its far reaching consequences. Here is further evidence for the origins of that outlook, confirming its debt to a medieval past.

There is also a third way in which these writers are of interest. They provide a fascinating example of the development of seventeenth-century English. They begin with the elaborate and baroque style of Rosse and develop through the cogent argument of Lawson and the hard-hitting metaphors of Bramhall, into the Swiftian mockery of Eachard, the invective of Whitehall and the clear prose of Clarendon. They make good reading for those who enjoy the literature of the seventeenth century, as well as for those concerned mainly with political ideas.

The following study is based on a course of lectures delivered at Wadham College, Oxford, in the Michaelmas Terms of 1948 and 1949.

In the composition of this book I am deeply indebted to the late Mr. Humphrey Sumner, Warden of All Souls, for his criticism and encouragement, and I should like to thank Professor A. P. d'Entrèves and Mr. H. R. Trevor-Roper for their advice in its initial stages. I am also indebted to the Rev. R. E. S. Hinde, Fellow and Chaplain of Hertford College; to Mr. G. A. Webb, Sub-Librarian of the Codrington Library, for his unfailing courtesy and assistance, and to the Delegates of the Clarendon Press for permission to quote from the works of Lord Clarendon.

JOHN BOWLE

Oxford
1950

HOBBES AND HIS CRITICS

CHAPTER I

THE CRITICS DESCRIBED

ONE aspect of the political writings of Hobbes has
been curiously neglected. While the implications
of the *De Cive* and the *Leviathan* have been fully
explored, and their effect on later political ideas often
examined, the impression which this formidable and
arrogant thinker made upon his contemporaries has been
comparatively little appreciated. Yet there is much to be
learnt from the impression a man makes on his own age.
And since Hobbes was original, and outside the main
stream of English political thought in the seventeenth
century, there is much to be gathered also from the widespread re-assertion of accepted principles which his
writings provoked.

For a full understanding of Hobbes it is necessary to
realize the startling impression he made on his contemporaries. One can see how shocked they were by him;
how strong their tradition was. Here, they insist, is a man
who questions basic assumptions; a ruthless critic of
immemorial institutions. As for his doubtful theological
opinions, an aspect of his thought which loomed largest
at the time, all the critics were unanimous that the
Leviathan was utterly subversive. Today the political
reaction to his ideas is more interesting. And all the critics
who form the subject of this study make the same assumption: this conceited and opinionated dogmatist, they
declare, undermines the solid institutions of England.

The *succès de scandale* that Hobbes' works enjoyed, with

their smart flavour of atheism, their up-to-date effect of demonstration, their fashionable 'method', provoked a re-assertion of the main English political tradition. It was made by representative men of talent, working in that tradition, not by one man of genius confounding Hobbes in some original way, and it reveals the assumptions such men took for granted.

And here the investigation shades into a theme of great historical interest: an examination of the background of the ideas behind Locke. New material from the Lovelace collection of Locke's papers has lately thrown fresh light on the origins, the implications and the importance of his thought.[1] Recent work, too, on the writings of Lawson and Hunton have shown how much Locke owed to men who were writing in the middle seventeenth century. And Lawson is one of the ablest of the critics of Hobbes. The challenge of Hobbes, indeed, was met by a restatement of a constitutionalism already rooted in English life and taken for granted — going back through Hooker, Fortescue, Bracton and John of Salisbury, far away into barbarian and Mediterranean Antiquity.

The contemporary critics of Hobbes form an interesting gallery, and a comparison of their views throws much light on the development of seventeenth-century political ideas. The manner of the attacks, for example, changes remarkably. The earlier critics were young men in the days of James I, brought up in the old school of rhetorical, semi-scholastic learning. They write, like Alexander Rosse and Bramhall, in the manner of Grotius and Sir Thomas Browne, piling up their recondite quotations in a

[1] See J. W. GOUGH, *John Locke's Political Philosophy*. Eight Studies. O.U.P. (1950).

riot of pedantry in the Jacobean style. They contrast
with the racy and colloquial dialogues of Dr. Eachard in
the 'seventies, the forensic skill of Whitehall, and the
lucidity of Clarendon's forceful argument.

I I

The critics selected have been taken in order of time
rather than of calibre, for it is interesting to follow how the
counter attack developed.

The first of them, Sir Robert Filmer, was born about
1588 and died in 1653.[1] Filmer was a royalist, a considerable scholar and a country gentleman of independent
mind. He was completely opposed to the views of Philip
Hunton and George Lawson, the forerunners of Locke.
In his *Anarchy of a Limited or Mixed Monarchy* (1648)
written against Hunton's *Treatise on Monarchie* (1643) and
its *Vindication* (1644), Filmer ably stated his position. But
he is best known to posterity as the victim of Locke, who
devoted the first of his two Treatises on Civil Government
to the ridicule and confutation of Filmer's *Patriarcha*, the
most diffuse and vulnerable of his works.

Since Filmer favoured patriarchal absolutism, his rather
perfunctory attack on Hobbes is not very effective, for
they were both authoritarians, if in different ways. The
pamphlet, entitled *Observations concerning the Originall of
Government*, runs to no more than fifty pages; twelve are

---

[1] His political works have recently been edited by Mr. Peter Laslett, who gives a full
account of Filmer's personality and background in his admirable introduction. See
Patriarcha and other Political Works of Sir Robert Filmer, Blackwell's Political Texts
(Oxford, 1949). See also J. W. ALLEN, 'Sir Robert Filmer', in *Social and Political Ideas
of some English Thinkers of the Augustan Age*, 1650-1750, ed. F. J. C. Hearnshawe,
chap. III. See also D. BUSH, *English Literature of the Earlier Seventeenth Century*. O.U.P.
(1945), pp. 236-7.

devoted to Hobbes. As one would expect, Filmer approves Hobbes' treatment of sovereignty, for he was an admirer and imitator of Bodin. 'With no small content,' he writes in his preface, 'I read Mr. Hob's book *De Cive* and his *Leviathan* about the rights of Sovereignty, which no man, that I know, hath so amply and judiciously handled.' But of the 'means of acquiring it', he thoroughly disapproves. 'It may seem strange that I should praise his building but mislike his foundations — but so it is.' 'His *Jus Naturae* and his Regnum Institutum', he concludes roundly, 'will not down with me.'

Filmer's pamphlet is vigorously written. Though sympathetic to Hobbes' views on sovereignty, he denies most of Hobbes' premises. He scouts the existence of a lawless State of Nature, which could not have occurred among the descendants of Adam, 'if God created Adam and of a piece of him made the woman, and if by Generation of them Two, as parts of them all mankind be propagated'. Nor is there any need for a war of all against all, save in conditions of exceptional famine. 'God was no such niggard at the creation.' And as for Hobbes' defence of the right of resistance, 'hereby', he says, 'any rogue or villain may murder his Sovereigne'. The rest of Filmer's argument follows the main position stated in his other works. It is not very considerable, but since the book was chronologically the first of the attacks on Hobbes, it will be worth a short examination. The author insists that sovereign power must of its nature be moral and absolute ('we do but flatter ourselves if we hope ever to be governed without an arbitrary power') since it can only be sanctioned by unlimited moral authority.[1] He has affinities

---

[1] Preface to *Anarchy of a Limited or Mixed Monarchy.*

with the old Tudor tradition of Conciliar government; something, therefore, in common with Clarendon. But he is not in line with the others, or with the preponderant opinion of the day. In more representative royalist circles the King's-power was held to be constitutional and bound by law.

III

Alexander Rosse is the next critic — a remarkable old character, something of a best seller in his day. He is the subject of the well-known couplet in *Hudibras*,

> There was an ancient sage philosopher
> That had read Alexander Rosse over.[1]

The point of the lines being that Rosse had written so much, and on such popular subjects. Nor did Rosse go unrewarded. Anthony Wood records his having made so much money from the sales of his works that a thousand pounds in gold was found between the leaves of his books — an interesting place to keep one's money.

Born at Aberdeen in 1591, and educated at the University there, this enterprising Scotsman, like many of his Jacobean contemporaries, had come south to seek his fortune, and succeeded in finding it. He had obtained the patronage of Edward Seymour, Earl of Hertford, the grandfather of William, later Marquis of Hertford and Duke of Somerset, who was to play so considerable a part in the Civil War, and through his patronage became Master of the Free School at Southampton and one of the chaplains to Prince Charles. Rosse subsequently became

---

[1] See SAMUEL BUTLER's *Hudibras*, canto II, lines 1-2.

Vicar of Carisbrooke in the Isle of Wight, and died in 1654, leaving substantial legacies to Southampton and to his native University at Aberdeen. He was a well-known controversialist in his day, a critic of Sir Kenelm Digby and a friend of Evelyn. He is buried at Bramshill, and at the church at Eversley, near Basingstoke, are two tablets to his memory.

He had not attained his comparative wealth merely by teaching the children of the southern English at Southampton. In 1634 he wrote the epic dedicated to young Prince Charles, called *Virgilius Evangelizans, Sive Historia Domini Nostri Jesu Christi Virgilianis Verbis et Versibius Descripta*. The fraudulent and plausible Scotch critic Lauder, whose forgeries and whose detection caused such a flutter in the mid-eighteenth century, accused Milton of plagiarizing from it, but the charge has no more justice than his other allegations.[1]

In 1649 we find Rosse translating the Koran out of French, prefaced by a 'Needful caveat or admonition'. In 1652 he had completed six volumes of a continuation of Sir Walter Raleigh's great History. They followed on *Some Animadversions and Observations upon Sir Walter Raleigh's Historie of the World, wherein his mistakes are noted and some doubtful passages cleared*. In this work he disagrees with Raleigh on the situation of the Ark.

[1] Lauder based his case on quotations in fact taken from Hog's Latin translation of Milton, but attributed to Masenius, a Professor at the Jesuit College in Cologne, who had written an epic on the Cosmos; to Grotius's *Adamus Exul*, and to Andrew Ramsey's poem on the creation of the world. He also cited Rosse. Milton, he says, 'gives an account of how the world was created . . . only now and then he enlarges beyond Grotius with the addition of hints and allusions taken from Ramsey, Du Bartas and Dr. Ross's *Virgilius Evangelizans* . . . Ross has spiritualized Virgil by making him speak like a Christian'. The epic was a comprehensive history of the Old and New Testaments. It began 'Arma Virumque Maro Cecinit, nos acta Deumque, Cedant Arma viro dum loquor acta Dei.' William Lauder, *An Essay on Milton's Use and Imitation of the Moderns in his Paradise Lost* (London, 1750), pp. 53, 94, 102.

'Sir Walter', he says, 'will not have the Ark to rest in Armenia as the received opinion is.' There are also sections on 'Hercules spinning' and 'Nebuchadnezzar truly transformed'. Raleigh, he argues, is again wrong: he maintains that Nebuchadnezzar lived and fed himself in the same manner as beasts, but that he was not changed in figure external. Nonsense, says Rosse, he was truly metamorphosed; it agrees more with the omnipotence of God. Besides, consider Lot's wife. Other characteristic topics are *'Noah* why Prometheus?' *'Vulcan* why the God of Mice?', *'Zoroaster* not Cham'.

This work he followed up in the next year with *Pansebia, or a View of All Religions,* and he wrote a work entitled *The Marrow of History* (1650). He was also a poet. In 1642 he had compiled *Mel Heliconium,* or Poetical Honey, an anthology of Scottish verse, and in 1647 published *Mystagogus Poeticus,* which went into six editions. The year before he had attacked the Galilean cosmology in a work entitled *The New Planet no Planet, or the earth no wandering star . . . here the earth's Immobility is Asserted.* There is also extant *Arcana Microcosmi, or the hid secrets of Man's Body disclosed, with a refutation of Doctor Browne's Vulgar Errors,* a work well worth investigation for amateurs of the seventeenth century.

It was natural that a publicist of such seniority and reputation should be one of the first to be called on to refute the *Leviathan.* His *Leviathan Drawn out with a Hook: or, Animadversions upon Mr. Hobbs his Leviathan,* appeared in 1653, when Rosse was sixty-two. The edition is bound up with the *Observations upon Sir Walter Raleigh's Historie of the World.* It is a short book of 102 pages.

The following extract from the Dedication, to Francis Lucy, Esquire, gives a fair specimen of his baroque early seventeenth-century style:

The Giant Goliah so affrighted the whole host of Israel by the vast bulk of his body, the weight and large dimensions of his spear and armor, with his defying and bragging words, that none of the Army durst encounter him. Only David, a Shepherd by profession in stature low, in years young, the least of all his brethren, and of meanest account among the people had the boldness to enter the lists with the uncircumcised Philistim. So I, a spiritual Shepherd by Profession, the least of the Tribe of Levi, little in mine own eyes and of small account in the world, observing how all the hosts of learned men in this Land look upon, but adventure not to buckle with Mr. Hobbs his Leviathan . . . have this summer set aside for a while my other studies to peruse this book and to detect some of his chief Tenets, which though erroneous and dangerous, are swallowed down by some young Sciolists without nauseating; which to me is a argument of great distemper in the mindes and affections of men . . . Methinks I see Religion and learning, Divinity and true Phylosophy, devotion and piety, for which this Island hath been glorious for many generations, saying, as the voice that the Christians heard in Jerusalem immediately before the destruction thereof, *Migremus hinc*. These are the Palladia, and as it were, the Tutelar Gods, by which th' British Empire hath so long stood, which if they forsake us, what are we else but a prey to our enemies?

After this admirable opening Rosse proceeds to address the reader.

Good Reader, David encountered with a Lion and a Bear; Daniel conversed among Lions; Paul fought with

Beasts at Ephesus, Hercules skirmished with an Ery-manthian Bear, a Nemæan Lion, a Lernæan Hydra; Aenæas drew his sword against the shaddows of Centaures, Harpies, Gorgons and Chimeras. But I have to do with a Strange Monster called Leviathan.

The full attack on *Leviathan* follows.

Here is the quaint idiom of Jacobean eloquence. There is also much good sense in Rosse's old-fashioned argument, which culminates by breaking into Latin for two pages, and quoting Scaliger, Carden,[1] Melanchthon (Epistola ad Eccium Cancellarium Bavaricum), Erasmus, Keckermanus,[2] Zanchius,[3] and Casaubon.

I V

The next critic, in chronological order, who deserves attention is Dr. Seth Ward, afterwards successively

[1] Carden, Girolamo (1501-76), mathematician, doctor and cosmographer; Professor of Medicine at Pavia 1543. His interests were wide: in 1551 he wrote *De Subtilitate Rerum*, and in 1557 *De Varietate Rerum*. He held pantheistic doctrines and anticipated ideas of the variety of species and adaptation to environment, though his learning was distorted by the astrological theories of his day.

[2] Keckerman, Bartholomeus (1571-1609), Calvinist theologian, polymath and systematizer. He was born at Danzig where he became a professor. He wrote and edited numerous works (e.g. on politics, *Disputationes.Practicae, nempe Ethicae, Œconomicae, Politicae, in Gymnasio Dantiscano* (Hanover, 1608); in English, *A Manducation to Theology, written in latin by Bartolomeus Keckermanus, done into English by T. Vicars* (undated, London, *c.* 1610)). Bayle says of him 'Il a composé un très grand nombre d'ouvrages, ou il fait paraître plus de méthode que d'esprit' *Dictionnaire Historique et Critique*). He is said to have plagiarized widely, and in turn to have suffered the same fate. Bayle's commentator remarks (edition 1820) 'J'ai rapporté ci-dessus la plainte d'un écrivain écossais (Donaldson) qui avait été volé par Keckermann. Un autre écossais (Andreas Aidius) fit tout le contraire; il vola Keckermann.'

[3] Zanchius, Hierome (1516-90), 'that eminent, grave and learned divine'. He was born at Alzano near Bergamo, and educated at the Lateran College. In 1550 he fled to Geneva and was appointed professor at Strasbourg in 1553-63, and Pastor of Chiavenne, Grisons; in 1568 he moved to Heidelberg. A tolerant Protestant, he refused to identify the Pope with Antichrist, 'Concordiae amans' (says his biographer, Melchior Adam) 'pacis ecclesiarum studiossissimus.' See his *Speculum Christianum*, translated H. Nelson (London, 1614).

Bishop of Exeter and Salisbury. He was a Fellow of Wadham from 1649 to 1659, during his tenure of the Savilian Professorship of Astronomy.

He wrote two criticisms of Hobbes. The first appeared in 1654 as an appendix to *Vindiciae Academiarum*;[1] the pamphlet itself is primarily an attack on a nonconformist preacher John Webster.[2] The second, addressed to Dr. John Wilkins, Warden of Wadham, was a criticism of Hobbes' philosophical position. It was entitled *In Thomae Hobbii Philosophiam Exercitatio Epistolica*[3] and appeared in 1656, being written in collaboration with Dr. Wallis, Hobbes' geometrical opponent. We are here only concerned with the first, which is an attack on Hobbes' attempt to impose uniformity of thought.

Ward was to be one of the ablest of the Restoration bishops, a worldly and striking personality who left his mark on both the dioceses he ruled. Born in 1617, he became a Fellow of Sidney Sussex, Cambridge, in 1640. He was ejected by the Puritans in 1644, but sufficiently made his peace with the rebels to obtain the Savilian Professorship in 1649. He was elected Principal of Jesus College, Oxford, in 1657, and President of Trinity College, Oxford, two years after, though he lost both appointments following a series of notable academic intrigues.

But he had been careful to keep in with the Royalists, and his appointment as Dean of Exeter in 1661 laid the

[1] *Vindiciae Academiarum, together with an appendix concerning what Mr. Hobbes and Mr. Dell have published in this argument* (Oxford, 1654, 65 pp.).

[2] John Webster (1610-82), Puritan Clergyman, surgeon and astrologer; Vicar of Mitton and preacher at All Hallows, Lombard Street. A prolific pamphleteer, he is best known for his attack on the belief in witches, *The Displaying of Supposed Witchcraft.*

[3] *Cui subjicitur Appendicula ad calumnias ab eodem Hobbio (in sex Documentis nuperrime editis) in authorem congestas, responsoria* (Oxon. 1656).

foundation of a wider career. In 1662 he succeeded a Wadham man, John Gauden, the probable author of *Eikon Basilike*, at Exeter, where he restored the cathedral and reorganized the finances. Translated to Salisbury in 1667, he embellished the cathedral and gave large sums towards improving the navigation of the Avon down to Christchurch. He founded the college for clergymen's widows which is still one of the architectural beauties of the north entrance to the close, and engaged in bitter controversy with Dr. Thomas Pierce, the Dean — a Wiltshireman from Devizes who had been President of Magdalen College, Oxford, and who was one of Hobbes' theological opponents.[1] We are here concerned with Ward as the Savilian Professor at Oxford, defending the intellectual freedom of the University. As an academic and scientific figure, rather than as a divine, Ward attacked Hobbes' attempt to force his doctrine on the Universities.

'I intend', he wrote in the ten pages of his criticism, 'to consider what he hath spoken of the Universities in his *Leviathan* . . . giving him leave to heare himselfe speake at large, (a thing he is infinitely taken with).'

v

Another of Hobbes' clerical critics was William Lucy, afterwards Bishop of St. David's, whose book appeared in 1657, three years after Ward's attack. Lucy had obtained the patronage of the Marquis of Hertford — the grandson of Rosse's patron, the Earl of Hertford. His lordship, says Lucy in the dedication, achieves in his

[1] The Rev. Thos. Pierce, *Autokatacrisis, with occasional Reflections on Master Hobbes* (1658).

own person the living refutation of Hobbes' doctrine of universal fear.

The book is entitled *Observations, Censures and Confutations of Diverse Errours in the* 12*th*, 13*th and* 14*th Chapters of Mr. Hobbs his Leviathan.* The author wrote under the pseudonym of William Pike, Christophilus. Like Rosse, he was connected with Hampshire, though where Rosse was an immigrant, Lucy was born at Hurstbourne, about five miles east of Andover, where the road from Basingstoke crosses the valley of the Test. He was the son of Sir Thomas Lucy, a local landowner, and Rosse had dedicated his book to Francis Lucy, probably a kinsman. Lucy was educated at Trinity College, Oxford, and at Caius, Cambridge. He had been chaplain to Buckingham, and he may well have met Rosse when he was chaplain to Prince Charles. In 1621 he became Rector of Burghclere and Highclere in Hampshire. He was an Arminian who suffered sequestration during the Interregnum. At the Restoration he was rewarded (insufficiently rewarded, he thought) with the notoriously ill-endowed Bishopric of St. David's. He called it 'the Poorest Bishopric in England and Wales'.

The book was, therefore, pseudonymously published in adverse circumstances. In the preface he remarks that 'he had been industrious to get learning, and in that time [before the civil war], like a Bee, laid up provision of books for mine old age; and sure, if it had pleased God to blesse that stocke, I had been encouraged to go on with my inquest. But His will was otherwise. My study abid the fate of better libraries and was rifled in those unhappy times of Warre, when to have anything was a crime'. Since that day, he continues, he had ceased to

24

buy books. The *Leviathan* came into his possession as a gift.

Lucy's pamphlet, though it contains many striking phrases, is not of very formidable calibre. In Aubrey's life of Hobbes, there is reference to him: ' "Theophilus Pike" (i.e. [William] Lucy, Bishop of St. Davids) who wrote *Observations, Censures and Confutations of Notorious Errours* in his *Leviathan*, 1664, but they are but weak ones,' — the comment by Wood. It may be that Wood was right, but Lucy is an eloquent representative of widespread average opinion.

V I

The Reverend George Lawson is the next of Hobbes' critics to be considered. Reference has already been made to his influence on Locke, which was considerable.[1] He represents quite a different school of thought from the High Church, old-fashioned Arminian doctrine, expressed with the complex erudition and rhetorical tropes fashionable in court circles in Jacobean and Caroline times. Lawson was a Puritan, an active opponent of the King. He was Rector of More in Shropshire, and he had already written, though he had not yet published, a treatise called *Politica Sacra et Civilis*. His book, which has a much more professional touch than the previous works considered, was published in the same year as Lucy's, in 1657. It is entitled *An Examination of the political part of Mr. Hobbs his Leviathan,* and runs to 214 pages of able, serious argument.

The tradition which Lawson represents owes much to

[1] See the article in which the debt of Locke to Lawson is fully discussed by Mr. A. H. Maclean, in the *Cambridge Historical Journal* (vol. IX, no. 1, 1947).

the lucidity and good sense of Hooker. He takes the orthodox line in defending the old conception of the Law of Nature, reflected in human affairs by Right Reason; but he moves in a world which is more modern, and in the long run intellectually more satisfying, than the entertaining, picturesque and discursive eloquence of the older tradition represented by Rosse and less forcibly by Lucy. Government, he declares, following the medieval argument coming down from scholastic thought and acclimatized in Elizabethan England by Richard Hooker, derives from the divine framework of the Universe. Hobbes' utilitarian outlook disgusts him. Thus 'To think that the sole or principle Cause of the constitution of a civil State is the consent of men, or that it aims at no further end than peace and plenty, is too mean a conceit of so noble an effect. And in this particular I cannot excuse Mr. Hobbs . . . and for this reason I undertake him.' 'Godliness and honesty' are the notes struck by this level-headed and clear argument, anticipating closely the ideas of Locke.

And here, while considering a forerunner of Whig tradition, it will be convenient to say a word about Philip Hunton.

Though he wrote as early as 1643, and cannot be ranged with the direct critics of the *Leviathan*, he falls into the same category as Lawson, and undoubtedly exercised some influence on Locke. His books are entitled *A Treatise of Monarchie, Done by an earnest Desirer of his Countries Peace,* and *A Vindication of the Treatise of Monarchy* (1644). They are both extraordinarily concise and able. The first consists of seventy-nine pages of concentrated argument, in style rather dry, but full of hard-hitting good sense and clear reasoning. *The Vindication*, his reply to royalist propaganda, and against the royalist's resort to arms shows similar qualities.

He came from the same neighbourhood as Lucy, being born at Andover in Hampshire, within a few miles of Hurstbourne, and his family had been previously settled at East Knoyle, west of Salisbury. This village is close to Dinton, the birthplace of Edward Hyde, first Earl of Clarendon, the most famous of Hobbes' critics. Since Hobbes himself came from Malmesbury in North Wilts., one may regard much of this whole controversy as being a matter of Wessex domestic concern, the intruding Scot, Rosse, being after all, naturalized at Southampton.

Hunton went up to Wadham in 1622. He later took Holy Orders and settled at Avebury in North Wilts. as a schoolmaster. Thence he moved to Devizes and Heytesbury; finally to the vicarage of Westbury. After a brief period of eminence as Provost of Cromwell's short-lived University College at Durham, he was ejected from Westbury in 1662. He supported himself by holding conventicles in the neighbourhood, and, sensibly enough, 'married a rich widow very late in life'. He died in 1682, aged 78.

His argument is extremely close to Locke's and fundamentally opposed to Hobbes' authoritarian outlook. 'For the end of Magistracie,' he writes, 'to set this out is no hard matter, if we consider what was looked at when God ordeyned it. That was the Good of the society of men over which it is set.' And, again, constitutional limited monarchy is not, he says, a 'stinted absolutism', but an authority conveyed by contract which has created the 'frame of government'. This position is similar to that of Locke, who maintains that contract creates civil society, not that there is contract between government and subjects. If government violates its trust, there is right of resistance since the frame of society has been dissolved.

VII

The next contributor to the counter-offensive provoked by the appearance of the *Leviathan* was an experienced and redoubtable controversialist.

John Bramhall, Bishop of Derry, afterwards Archbishop of Armagh, possessed a style which was both hard-hitting and picturesque. He was born in 1594, in the same year as Lucy, of a substantial family in Cheshire. Like Seth Ward, he was educated at Sidney Sussex, Cambridge, a college which afterwards harboured Cromwell. In 1623 he became Chaplain to Tobias Mathew, Archbishop of York, and accompanied Wentworth in the same capacity to Ireland. Here, in 1634, he became Bishop of Derry. In 1641 he fled to England and put his services and his plate at the disposal of the King. He was long in exile in France, Germany and the Low Countries, and he met and argued with Hobbes in Paris.[1] He found this controversy, he says, 'sportive occupation'. In 1660 he was nominated to the Archbishopric of Armagh, and formally appointed in January 1661. He died in 1663. His book is entitled *The Catching of the Leviathan, or the Great Whale*. It appeared in 1658, the

---

[1] The best short account of his personal contacts and controversy with Hobbes is in Sir Leslie Stephen's biography of Hobbes (English Men of Letters series).

year after Lawson's and Lucy's contribution to the counter-offensive. It is bound up with his larger *Castigation of Mr. Hobbes*, which is concerned with theology and with metaphysical arguments about Free Will, an attack to which Hobbes' reply will be found in his collected works.[1]

Bramhall was an extremely able man of business; a worldly prelate who had done well for himself in a hard school of controversy with Southern Irish Catholics and Ulster Protestants. His book is in style half way between the picturesque eloquence of Rosse and the more modern lucidity of Eachard, Clarendon and Whitehall.

Bishop Vesey, in his account of Bramhall's controversy with Hobbes, calls Hobbes' writings 'the brutish doctrines of the supercilious dogmatist' (a phrase which can stand comparison with the modern 'deviationist pig'), and describes him as a 'very natural philosopher whose doctrines have had so great a share in the debauching of this generation'. After calling Hobbes a 'Pander to Bestiality', he concludes — 'Yet . . . the Catching of the Leviathan hit him hard . . . and although this great Leviathan takes pleasure in that deluge of Atheism he hath spewed out of his mouth and rouls with great wantonness in the Deep, attended by a numerous shoal of his own spawning, yet the hook is still in his Nose. Good judges have thought he hath not licked himself well of those wounds the Bishop of Derry gave him.'

A modern assessment confirms Vesey's opinion. With trenchant good sense, Bramhall goes to the root of Hobbes' argument on the crucial points of Natural Law, the State of Nature and of Sovereignty. Though he is

[1] See Molesworth's edition of Hobbes' works, vol. IV.

sometimes hot-headed and violent, Bramhall's examination
stands high, for polemical force, in the counter-attack.

VIII

The most homely and the most entertaining of the
writers under review was the Reverend John Eachard,
who belonged to a generation much younger than those
so far mentioned. He was born in 1636, over forty years
after Bramhall, and he became Master of St. Catherine's
Hall at Cambridge in 1675. At the age of thirty-four he
had already published an anonymous, racy and convincing
examination of the *Grounds and Occasions of the Contempt
of the Clergy*. By this forceful and trenchant pamphlet
he is best known. But although this work is extremely
sensible, with its candid, practical criticism of the over
linguistic and pedantic university curriculum of the day —
(why, he asks, cannot the prospective country parson be
grounded in the literature of his own tongue?) — and in
its harrowing anatomy of the shifts and anxieties with
which the poorer clergy were beset, it does not compare
in range and content with his little-known criticism of
Hobbes.

The book is in two volumes, published successively in
1672 and 1673. The first volume is entitled *Mr. Hobbes'
state of Nature Considered in a Dialogue between Philautus
and Timothy*.[1] The second is larger; *Some opinions of Mr.
Hobbes Considered in a second dialogue between Philautus
and Timothy*.[2]

Eachard had a great knack of colloquial satire. He
always keeps to the most homely similes, and his dialogue

[1] 165 pp.   [2] 309 pp.

often runs like the shrewd and rapid conversation of some hard-bitten old farmer. He belongs to quite another school to the learned, complex rhetoric of Rosse and Bramhall, having more of an eighteenth-century tang about his earthy good sense. In his dedication of the books to Archbishop Sheldon, he apologizes for this apparently frivolous technique. He maintains that if Hobbes' arguments are boiled down to their essentials and stripped of their glamour of phrase, their virulence is greatly diminished. By thus reducing them, he maintains, one gets a juster view of Hobbes' limitations. Secondly, he continues, he wants to appeal to worldly young men who affect a Hobbesian outlook out of devilment and who will not bother to read pedantic arguments. This objective Eachard was well qualified to achieve. His dialogue is consistently racy and amusing, yet it goes to the root of Hobbes' argument. It is curious that the book is so little known, for from the literary aspect alone it is remarkable.

The work is, indeed, too long, but its better passages are rewarding. Eachard, for example, has an eye for the behaviour of children and animals. He fetches his instances from the more obvious, not to say sordid, aspects of life. This is done deliberately, to counteract what he regards as the 'magisterial pomposity' of Hobbes. In an admirable passage he translates one of Hobbes' most resounding and apparently convincing periods into plain speech, juxtaposing his own version with the original. Here is an example of his method and phrasing:

Philautus (Hobbes) remarks on children's propensity to quarrel. Their desire to fight, he says, and 'scratch poore nurse', demonstrates their natural disposition to war.

Timotheus replies sarcastically, 'Yes, I've seen the whole porringer of sweetened milk, with its toppling white bread, rouling up and down the uncertaine floore, and the little state of Nature, as hard worrying the righteous and inoffensive Nurse as ever poor dogge was worried by Hare.'

Again, government, he argues, is not necessary because all men are wicked, but because of a minority of criminals, and because of the ordinary accidents of life. It is as well, for example, not to leave the dairy door open. 'For who knows, but, of a sudden, a sowe, having small scruples about Meum and Tuum, may rush in with her train of little thoughts and, invading the milk bowls, should rejoice in the confusion.' 'Train of little thoughts' is an authentic touch. But Eachard was no mere buffoon. His argument is sound, and his sketch of the behaviour of four individuals dropped upon an imaginary island, convincing. It is called the Isle of Pines; Roger, Dick, Towser and Tumbler are the characteristic names of the islanders.

IX

The best known of Hobbes' opponents, and the name with by far the greatest contemporary prestige, is Edward Hyde, first Earl of Clarendon. He brings the judgment of a statesman of great experience to bear on Hobbes even more effectively than Bramhall, who comes nearest to him in knowledge of affairs. His book is much the most dignified, thorough and comprehensive of those under review. But, as Charles II found, Clarendon can sometimes be tedious.

In 1667 he had fallen from power and fled overseas. The book appeared in 1676: it is gravely and portentously entitled *A Brief view and Survey of the Dangerous and pernicious Errors to Church and State, in Mr. Hobbes' Book entitled Leviathan.* It is dedicated to Charles II and was written from Clarendon's place of exile at Moulins, a place in the country near Nevers on the Loire, about 120 miles south of Paris, well away from the attentions of Clarendon's English enemies. The old statesman had solaced his exile by the systematic confutation of Hobbes, a reputable and well-thought-of task. It is a longish book of 322 pages, and follows out the scheme of the *Leviathan,* going through it systematically and relentlessly.

Clarendon's treatment shows a balanced judgment and a fine sense of proportion; his argument is powerfully set out. The same qualities of style which distinguish his great *History* and his autobiography are displayed when he deals with this less congenial theme. Further, as he develops his criticism, Clarendon's point of view about government becomes apparent. It confirms the generally accepted view of him as a belated Elizabethan, desiring a benevolent monarchy ruling through Conciliar government, and regarding the concessions made by the King as given, not out of obedience to the Whiggish theory of contract, but by 'condescent of grace' — in order that government may proceed harmoniously.

One cannot, then, group Clarendon either with the academic critics of the earlier generation (though he has affinities with Filmer), or with the Whig outlook of Hunton and Lawson. Rather his criticism of Hobbes is typical of a Conservative statesman of the old order. As such, it has dignity, insight and value. He points out, as he is well entitled to do, that Hobbes has had no experience of public business and held no responsible posts. His 'theorem' of government, for all its vaunted realism, is, therefore, academic and unreal. 'I should be very glad', he concludes in the closing paragraph of his book, 'that Mr. Hobbes might have a place in Parliament, and sit in Counsel, and be present in Courts of Justice, and other Tribunals, whereby it is probable he would find, that his solitary cogitations, how deep soever, and his too peremptory adhering to some Philosophical Notions, and even Rules of Geometry, have misled him in the investigation of Policy.'

Clarendon's book has not, perhaps, the immediate appeal of the rhetorical quaintness of Rosse, or the homeliness of Lucy, the constructive power of Lawson or the spectacular invective of Bramhall, still less of the brisk dialogues of Eachard, but as a solid and well weighed criticism it is of permanent value. Yet even in the University Clarendon so much loved,[1] this aspect of

[1] See the letter of resignation from Clarendon to the Vice-Chancellor of Oxford University:

Good Mr. Vice-Chancellor,

Having found it necessary to transport myself out of England, and not knowing when it will please God that I shall return again, it becomes me to take care, that ye University may not be without the service of a Person able to be of more use to them than I am likely to be; and I do therefore hereby surrender ye office of Chancellor into ye hands of ye said University, to ye end, that they may make choice of some other Person, better qualified to assist and protect them, than I am: I am sure He can never be more affectionate to it. I desire you, as ye last suit I am like to make of you, to believe that I do not fly my country for guilt; and how passionately soever I am pursued, that I have not done anything to make the University ashamed of me or to refute the good opinion they had once of me. And though I must have no further mention in your public Devotions, which I have always exceedingly valued, I hope I shall always be remembered in your private prayers as,

Good Mr. Vice-Chancellor,
Your affectionate servant,
CLARENDON

Calice this (7.17) *Dec.* 1667

his writings, overshadowed by his fame as an historian, has hitherto not been much appreciated.

X

The last of Hobbes' critics to be considered is a lawyer: a man of the world, and of the Restoration world at that. Able, rather coarse, on the make, he is the least high-minded of them all. And his case is clear, representative, ordinary and powerful. It links, deliberately, the memories of Cromwell's arbitrary rule with the threat of contemporary Catholic conspiracy. It appeared at the height of the scare over the Popish Plot in 1679, the year of Hobbes' death.

Whitehall supplements the others, rounds them off by giving a lawyer's point of view. His book was occasioned by the threat of arbitrary government implied by the Duke of York's Catholic ambitions, by the questions of succession and exclusion, then at fever-heat owing to the fear of the Popish Plot. He sees Hobbes' argument in terms of current politics: as originally put forward to justify Oliver's rule of the sword in 1651 and as potentially dangerous in justifying the arbitrary rule of a Catholic king. Whitehall affirms in trenchant phrases the supremacy of the law, and ends by quoting some of Aristotle's most valuable opinions.

The Leviathan Found Out; or the Answer to Mr. Hobbes's Leviathan, In that which my Lord of Clarendon hath past over. by John Whitehall . . . Barrister at Law, runs to 163 pages.[1]

[1] Printed by A. Godbid and J. Playford, dwelling in Little Britain, London, 1679.

On the title page is ironically displayed the motto used by Hobbes himself. Job xli. 33, *Non est potestas Super Terram quae comparetur ei*, 'Upon Earth there is not his Like . . .' The whole argument hangs on this phrase, quoted at its beginning and at its culmination. The Leviathan, says Whitehall, is indeed like nothing on earth; a monstrosity, horrifying to God and man.

The book is dedicated to the Rt. Honourable Heneage Lord Finch, Baron of Daventry, Lord High Chancellor of England, and in the dedicatory epistle Whitehall's legal qualifications and connections are stressed. He is writing, he insists, as a barrister, qualified by his education in the Inner Temple to supplement the arguments of Lord Daventry's 'Noble Predecessor, my Lord of Clarendon'. He will deal with matters passed over by Clarendon 'as ridiculous in themselves and not worthy of his Pen, he intending as I suppose only to Answer his Civil Politics'. Daventry's example has taught him that it is 'the duty of every good man to indeavour the support of the government he was protected by'. 'Whereupon,' he continues, 'my lord, I having . . . got a sight of it' (the *Leviathan*) was 'as much surprised with the obliquity of it as the Queen of Sheba (may I make Sacred contrasts by illustration) with the wisdom of Solomon'. He felt that the case made against Hobbes was not enough, for Hobbes subverted not only 'faithful subjection' but property. This defence of property is fundamental to Whitehall's argument. He followed up his book in the following year by a shorter work, entitled *Behemoth Arraigned, or a Vindication of Property against a Fanatical Pamphlet stiled Behemoth, or the History of the Civil Wars of England from* 1640-1660. *subscribed by Tho: Hobbes of Malmesbury.*[1]

The implications of Hobbes' argument, he insists, are appalling. Not only does he undermine allegiance and property, but he has launched a 'Mahometan indeavour by ill words to surplant the greatest part of civil learning'. So Whitehall has employed the long vacation to express his loyalty to the government, which he has 'for so long lived peaceably under', and 'to make it manifest to the world — (to prevent further mistakes in that matter) — that under the name Leviathan are contained the most horrid and execrable opinions that were ever suffered to see the light in any Christian Kingdom . . . tending to extirpation of all sense of religion in the minds of men (which is the basis of Government)'. The book, he says later, is 'as full of damnable opinions as a toad is of poison'. Whitehall's attack, which is primarily an occasion to denounce the Catholics, is distinguished throughout by political rancour, pitched high by the critical situation in the year following the first revelations of the 'Popish Plot' and by the author's desire to ingratiate himself with the government. It also deals fully with the religious aspect of the *Leviathan*. Like Clarendon, he traverses the book point by point, and his treatment is determined by the proportions of his adversary's argument. Out of 163 pages, nearly half are devoted to Hobbes' Theology, though Whitehall sums up ably at the end, giving full weight to the political and legal questions with which he is best able to deal. Though Whitehall is a royalist, and no Whig, the book forms part

[1] By J. Whitehall, Barrister at law; London 1680. It is dedicated to Prince Rupert and runs to 92 pages.

of the constitutionalist attack on Hobbes, and, through Hobbes, on the threatened arbitrary power of a Catholic Monarchy. Far less temperate than Lawson, he has something of Eachard's colloquial vigour: yet where Eachard is bantering and playful, the London barrister is out to win his case. There is little of the dignity and poise of Clarendon, and Whitehall is far from the more gracious academic atmosphere of Rosse and Lucy. Yet the similarity of his argument is remarkable. Where Rosse and Lucy quote Aristotle, so does Whitehall: where Lawson insists on the rule of law, and Bramhall on the implications of Hobbes' 'taking his sovereign for better and not for worse', Whitehall, the man of affairs, unmasks the practical implications of Hobbes' argument. And, like Clarendon, he pins it down to Hobbes' personal situation in 1651. Whitehall wants to raise the bogy of Oliver's standing army in the critical situation of 1679. These points are hammered home with a forensic skill. Obvious, rancourous and able, John Whitehall speaks for the legal and commercial interests who were the backbone of the combined resistance to James II, and victors of the struggle of 1688.

XI

Such were the principal contemporary political critics of Hobbes. They are remarkably interesting, both as political theorists, and as representatives of seventeenth-century opinion. Their books and their background lead into county history, into the byways of contemporary literature. They contribute to a detailed picture of the seventeenth century.

How far can one discern a pattern of ideas common to them all? How far, for the political theorist, are these criticisms of Hobbes significant? These questions are worth investigation. And here, perhaps, where political theory and history meet (as they ought to do), and when thought emerges so clearly from the context of its time, fundamental and urgent questions of political thought may be illuminated.

CHAPTER II

HOBBES RECONSIDERED

BEFORE taking account of Hobbes' first two critics, Sir Robert Filmer and Alexander Rosse, and plunging into the seas of seventeenth-century polemical erudition, it will be worth taking stock of Hobbes' position at the time, and recapitulating briefly the development and significance of his thought.

The radical innovation which Hobbes made in political theory is generally familiar. The assumptions of political theorists had hitherto been moral and theological. According to Plato and Aristotle, the aim of the state had been to promote the good life, if only for a minority. Government had been theoretically subordinated to an ethical purpose, and law justified as the means of bridling the lust for arbitrary power which made the rule even of enlightened princes dangerous. Cicero, inspired by Stoic ideas, had maintained that government reflects a divinely sanctioned cosmic order, ascertainable by reason, which all men possess. Whatever its practical shortcomings, the political theory of Antiquity was moral and universal. It centred on the betterment, the endurance or the glorification of life. The vitality of the great civilization it reflected and inspired can still be sensed in the literature, art and architecture which embodied the august ideal of *romanitas* and the prosperity of the Mediterranean world.

With the gradual spread of Christianity, political thought no longer centred so directly on the concerns of life; it began to centre upon the revelation of God. For St. Augustine, government is no longer splendid; it is a necessary evil, *remedium peccatorum*. But it is sanctified as part of a God-ordained order, necessary for the world so long as men persist in sin. By the early eleventh century in the West, government was becoming in theory the secular arm of a universal Church. Medieval thought, moreover, a synthesis of Christian and pagan ideas, was reinforced by ancient barbarian concepts of the limitation of kingly power, and by feudal ideas of contract. In spite of the practical incompetence, the poverty and widespread illiteracy of the Middle Ages, the fundamental idea of a cosmopolitan Christian commonwealth had dominated the Western European world.

With the gradual breakdown and transformation of medieval civilization and the emergence of dynastic states claiming sovereignty, the universality of political thought declined. But the idea of commonwealth on a limited scale persisted; for example, in England in the writings of Fortescue in the late fifteenth century, and of Hooker in the last decade of the Elizabethan Age. It was also transmitted to the seventeenth-century Radicals of whom Lilburne was the prophet, while, on a much more influential level, Hooker's ideas were secularized and broadened by the Whig forerunners of Locke. This great tradition, with its unbroken continuity from Antiquity and medieval times, was destined to achieve a world-wide influence owing to the effect of Locke's writings in England, France and North America. The ideal of constitutional commonwealth, of self government under the law, has been embodied in formidable institutions and has proved in practice the basis of the most successful kind of government. Its inspiration had from the beginning been moral and religious.

Today, one of the most urgent problems of political thought is whether it is possible, with the decline of religious and metaphysical belief, and in face of the vast problems of modern mass civilization and modern science, to maintain and adapt the integrity and the vigour of this old and powerful tradition.

Hobbes was the first to attack its fundamental assumption in an elaborate way. He attempted to provide a materialist psychological and sociological foundation for a new political theory, based on the assumption that human conduct was determined, as the conduct of ants and bees is determined, by reflex actions following known laws. He set himself against all the powerful and still developing constitutionalist tradition, expressed in innumerable books and long entrenched in institutions. He was a radical sceptic, with a cynical view of human nature. If he was not an atheist, he was certainly an agnostic. Hobbes was more of a materialist than Descartes. Both were rationalist and anti-scholastic, but whereas Descartes stood for dualism, Hobbes was a materialist: for Descartes there were two substances, mind and matter, but for Hobbes matter and motion alone were real. As Cudworth remarked, 'A modern atheistic pretender to wit hath publicly owned this same conclusion that "mind is nothing but local motion in the organic parts of man's body".'[1] Henry More made it his business 'to root out this sullen conceit' of Hobbes 'That the very Notion of a Spirit or Substance Immaterial is . . . pure

[1] See R. CUDWORTH, *True Intellectual System*, Tegg (1845), vol. III, p. 418, quoted by BASIL WILLEY in *The Seventeenth Century Background*, Chatto (1934), p. 156. Also F. BRANDT, *Thomas Hobbes' Mechanical Conception of Nature* (1928) pp. 379-82.

Non-sense'. He calls Hobbes 'that confident exploder of *Immaterial Substances* out of the world'.[1]

Holding this outlook, Hobbes tried to sweep away the whole structure of traditional sanctions, and to set up a new and raw standard by which government should be judged — utility. Anticipating Bentham and Austin, he wished to base social morality simply on positive law. The objective, he believed, is not the pagan 'good life' or Christian 'salvation'; it is a state of mind, 'felicity'. That felicity is hard to define. Professor Oakeshott has wrestled with the task in an introduction to the *Leviathan*.[2] Whatever precisely the idea meant to Hobbes, it was anthropocentric, conceived within the bounds of immediate experience. Something, like the 'pleasure' of the Utilitarians, to be obtained by calculation: and it can be brought about only if society is deliberately contrived to circumvent the results of greed and selfishness, motives which he thought predominant in human nature.

Since, in Hobbes' view, the traditional religious and ethical means of changing men's hearts from within have to be discarded, it is necessary to create an external knave-proof and fool-proof structure which will prevent their behaviour having its normal consequences. As Mr. Plamenatz has well written of Hobbes, 'the state, according to him, is neither the promoter of the good life, nor the protector of rights. It is the conciliator of interests'. One might add, the forcible conciliator.[3] Hobbes' outlook was, therefore, utilitarian and he may be regarded as a forerunner of the Benthamite school of

[1] See H. MORE, *Immortality of the Soul*, quoted by WILLEY, op. cit., p. 162.
[2] *Hobbes's 'Leviathan'*, edited with an Introduction by M. Oakeshott (Blackwell's Political Texts, Oxford, 1946).
[3] See J. P. PLAMENATZ, *The English Utilitarians*, Blackwell (1949), p. 15.

political thought; but he differed profoundly from Bentham and his followers in believing that the remedy for greed and egotism was authoritarian government. For though Hobbes' originality lies in his definition of the unqualified nature of sovereign power, irrespective of its form, he shows a consistent liking for authoritarian methods.

This revolutionary attitude rested on the assumptions of a crude behaviourism. First, that we can know directly nothing of reality. Mind is 'but a mere whiffling, evanid and fantastic thing; so that the most absolutely perfect of all things in the universe is grave, solid, and substantial senseless matter'.[1] In consequence the metaphysical and religious sanctions of traditional political thought are moonshine. This view, of course, is not explicitly stated, but it is implied. Secondly, he believed that we know 'felicity' when we see it. Thirdly, he believed that the best way of attaining 'felicity' is by the 'conciliation of interests' within his crude blue-print for authoritarian government. And his arrogant and powerful mind could seriously recommend this programme to princes, in the hope that they would convert it into reality. Like Marx, he claimed to give a 'scientific' explanation of human behaviour, which he regarded as determined by reflex actions, and to provide a political theory which was based on conduct so determined.

Though Hobbes' crude materialism has been undermined by the discoveries of modern physics and the development of modern philosophy,[2] he was clearly a

[1] Cudworth; quoted by WILLEY, op. cit., p. 155.
[2] See A. N. WHITEHEAD, *Science and the Modern World* for 'the fallacy of misplaced concreteness'. See also GILBERT RYLE, on the 'Ghost in the Machine', in *The Concept of Mind* (London, 1950).

writer of great and original importance. The trenchant genius of this seventeenth-century Wiltshireman, expressed with brutal disregard for the feelings and beliefs of his contemporaries, had raised a fundamental question. If his scepticism is even partially justified, how are we to maintain the creative vitality and the decencies of civilized society? His gloomy picture of human limitations may be wrong, but he had the courage and insensibility to paint it.

On the other, political, level, there is little doubt that Hobbes was unpractical. Even if the state has the purely utilitarian function he suggests, it is very doubtful if the precarious authoritarian government which he advocates will long attain even this limited aim, nor, devoid of any *mystique*, would it be psychologically satisfying. In practice a self-governing commonwealth under law succeeds much better in this purpose, though in backward societies absolutism may be a necessary expedient. Even if the metaphysical and religious sanctions of classical and medieval political theory have to be written off, there is every reason to suppose, from the historical and sociological evidence, that the tried expedients of constitutional government, if men can be induced to practise them, will better promote 'felicity' than the cruder patterns of power. Today the dangers of the abuse of power by modern Leviathans are familiar and menacing. If civilized government is impossible without the religious sanctions which originally contributed to bring it into being, there seems little hope that a modern version of Hobbes' stark utilitarianism will prove a way out. No society can survive without its myth. The Hobbesian State would be without one.

But Hobbes was the first to raise this formidable question: given a radical scepticism about natural law and a cosmic order, how can society continue to believe in itself, how retain its vitality? To be the first to pose this question was a formidable achievement; and it is to this that Hobbes owes his renown. But Hobbes never found the political or psychological answer. He was a pioneer philosopher and a prince of heretics, but he was not a statesmanlike writer. He is the prophet of crude expedients in government, which tend to gross abuse of power. Hobbes was important because he had the courage, or the rashness, to break away from all the old ideas. This his contemporaries understood. It will be apparent from their writings how completely they were steeped in the old, psychologically satisfactory, traditions, and how well they realized what seemed to them the atrocious implications of the new point of view. They were shocked by his depreciation of government into a mere convenience. 'It is', says Lawson, 'too mean a conceit for so noble an effect.' They fully understand the vistas of confusion which the loss of the old certainties would entail. The traditional outlook had already lost its universality with the decline of medieval Christendom and the emergence of nation states: Hobbes threatened it with the loss of its moral and religious sanctions as well. His critics' therefore concentrated their attack on the fundamental implications of Hobbes' thought, which are well brought out in the controversy. It will not be amiss for modern admirers of Hobbes to be reminded what the implications are. As Lord Lindsay remarks, he saw 'with great clearness and honesty everything in human conduct which one without faith and emotion can see'.[1]

---

[1] A. D. LINDSAY, *Hobbes' Leviathan*, Everyman ed., p. xi.

The critics concentrated, also, on his weakness as a practical statesman, and here they were on strong ground. Their works explain why it was fortunately Locke, and not Hobbes, who spoke for the England of 1688 and of the eighteenth century. Here is the basis of Whig constitutionalism in the making, a representative cross-section of opinion in a nation which was to lead the world in the practice of politics. But before turning to his critics, it is worth examining further the development of Hobbes' ideas.

I I

Hobbes' first work had been his translation of Thucydides, undertaken while he was in his early period of residence with the Cavendish family, and completed in 1628. He was already forty when it appeared, and he had behind him a long period of classical and scholastic studies. He had been influenced by Aristotle though he seems to have remained impervious to the profound insight of the *Politics*. And, as Professor Oakeshott points out, he was deeply versed in late medieval thought.[1] He had been abroad in France, Germany and Italy. He was to follow up these foreign contacts in 1629, and again from 1634 to 1637.

During the 'thirties, the bent of his independent and powerful mind had been increasingly materialistic. Two strata of development seem apparent in his writings — a classical and scholastic idiom strangely combined with mechanical rationalism, the characteristic and original quality of the latest seventeenth-century thought.

[1] See M. OAKESHOTT, op. cit., introduction.

Although, as has been emphasized, he disagreed with fundamental aspects of the Cartesian position, going much further along the materialist and behaviourist road,[1] he was deeply influenced by the Cartesians. Steeped in this new outlook, his mind was too powerful, too capable of vast synthesis, too confident, to be content with keeping his opinions to himself or making them a mere hobby. He attempted a fantastically ambitious synthesis. While so many of his contemporaries, their minds running into grooves of detailed scholarship, were concerned with the creation of a universal language, or content with amateurish experiment, Hobbes' ambition was to reconcile old nominalist scholastic ideas with a new mechanical outlook in both philosophy and politics.[2] He was concerned with the ultimate questions of life. He was determined to set out his independent and original conclusions in a series of works touching all aspects of human experience.

Hobbes' ideas took long to mature. Most men of outstanding ability show it young: their early work is often their freshest and most original, and starts themes afterwards elaborated. Yet this morose genius pondered the conclusions of decades of study, and of wide experience of cities and men, before he set down his view of political life in a systematic psychological way which was without precedent.

It is worth remembering that personally Hobbes had been relatively sheltered. He had not been forced to measure himself against men of action in the cut and thrust of predatory commerce or in politics or administration. He had held no formidable responsibility; made no

[1] See his *Objections* to Descartes, 1641.
[2] For the unconscious assumptions behind Hobbes' thought see B. WILLEY, op. cit., chap. VI.

great decisions. Though largely emancipated from the conventions of current academic expression, he remained essentially bookish, a man of the study.

Yet he was forced to turn his mind to public affairs. His first work on politics, written in 1640, in the year of the impeachment of Strafford and of Laud, was occasioned by the crisis leading up to the Civil War — an event which determined his whole outlook in the way that modern thinkers are conditioned by the greater wars of our own time. By 1640 Hobbes was fifty-two. His mind, with its original and dogmatic power, was formed. He had grown up and come to maturity in much more propitious circumstances. The 'thirties had appeared to many of the upper classes — to Clarendon for example — as a time of ease and prosperity. Hobbes' life had been sheltered, smooth, spent in congenial surroundings. Yet this ferocious intellect first came into its own when the political gales were rising. The 'Crowe' ('the black crowe' as he had been called in his schooldays because of his dark hair), uttered his first warning against a stormy sky. What Lord Lindsay calls his 'genial sarcasm' was to be reinforced with an urgent and confident diagnosis and a plan of action.

His book was entitled *The Elements of Law, Natural and Politic*. Though it was not printed until the Civil Wars were over, the King murdered, the Commonwealth in being, it was written by 1640. Its immediate audience had been Falkland's circle at Great Tew. This short work is divided into two sections — 'On Human Nature or the Fundamental Elements of Policy' and 'De Corpore Politico'. The first states Hobbes' agnostic and materialist position; the second its political consequences.

Here Hobbes is attempting a real sociology. He sees

society, with his penetrating and crude vision, as a whole. He is determined to relate his politics to his philosophy. He was attempting nothing less than to deduce a political philosophy from deterministic assumptions which made men appear automata, devoid of free will.

This agnostic attitude was radically opposed to the whole tradition of the orthodox political thought of his contemporaries. Here was a man with the courage to set out in plain terms the consequences of a sceptical world-outlook. In that time such an outlook was revolutionary. It was to influence, directly and indirectly, the development of thought for four centuries.

As Professor Willey has pointed out, Hobbes assumes that motion was the ultimate reality, as far as man can apprehend it. Yet the strength of his position was not in its positive assumptions, but its negative and courageous statement of the unfathomed mystery of life. Most of the ideas of the *Leviathan* can be found already expressed in pithy and concentrated form in this small volume, so clearly and trenchantly arranged, written ten years earlier, though actually printed only a year before the appearance of his greater work.

Here are already the following propositions: (i) the state of nature is a state of war; every man has a right to all things by natural right, an assumption which cuts across the whole orthodox tradition of natural law and a benevolent cosmic order; (ii) the surrender of natural right by mutual covenant; (iii) the setting up of a sovereign power on a purely utilitarian basis; (iv) subordination of ecclesiastical to civil power; (v) the right of the subject to transfer allegiance if the sovereign fails in his primary task, the maintenance of security.

Such arguments were likely to be unpopular with the lawyers as well as the clergy: among the conservative lawyers, because of their concern with inherited Divine Right; and among the parliamentary lawyers, the constitutionalists, because of their concern with the 'ancient fundamental laws', with a largely mythical Anglo-Saxon freedom 'before the Norman ingress', and with a reinterpretation of the medieval concept of contract as the basis of civil society. Their adversary had already tried to turn one of their principle weapons against themselves.

Hobbes, then, had made up his mind about politics. He was fifty-two, and England was heading for civil war. That year he took himself off to France. Settled in Paris, Hobbes had further elaborated his political ideas. The basic arguments of the *Elements of Law, Natural and Politic* were worked out more fully in the *De Cive*, the Latin treatise published in 1642. Most of it was to be translated into English in 1651, under the title of *Philosophical Rudiments concerning Government and Society*. Hitherto, then, Hobbes had been very chary of publicly committing himself. *The Elements of Law*, 1640, and the *De Cive* in translation, in which his position was fully formulated, did not come into wide circulation until 1650 and 1651, respectively. And in the latter year the full attack was to be launched in the *Leviathan*.

The *De Cive* makes quite as good reading as the *Leviathan*, and the translation (the *Philosophical Rudiments*) shows the same trenchant and arresting command of language. The fundamental position remains unchanged, as stated in the early 'Elements of Policy' — the state of nature; the utilitarian contract and the rest.

The years in Paris were spent mainly in philosophical

51

and mathematical study and discussion. Hobbes became mathematical initiator to Prince Charles, who afterwards befriended him. But the close and quarrelsome little society of refugees which descended on Paris after the defeat of the King's cause must have been singularly tedious. Hobbes, moreover, had offended French and Anglican clerical opinion. And he was now getting on for sixty. He had set to and written the great treatise that was to make him famous.

So Hobbes returned to his own country. He may well have thought that now the Civil Wars were apparently decided, the lesser of two evils was to return to his Cavendish patrons, whose establishment had weathered the political storm. It may be that he might have wanted to conciliate Cromwell, already, though his position as Protector was not yet formally established, the most powerful man in the state. It seems likely that Hobbes, at the age of sixty-three, was determined to put his case, and by a cumulative publicity (the three books all coming together in three years) to state the truth about life and politics as he saw it. It may well have seemed now or never. He could not know that he was to live to be ninety-one.

The age was one of hectic political debate. As is well known, all points of view were being widely and often irresponsibly canvassed in the revolutionary conditions of the years following the King's death. Into this medley of pamphlet warfare and religious fanaticism swept the *Leviathan*; modern, lucid, apparently realistic; comprehensive, based on the latest materialistic psychology, barbed with trenchant and memorable epigrams, the work of a phrase-maker of the first order, of a mind powerful, original, ruthless. To those who accepted the argument Hobbes appeared to be a genius, one who had cut down to the roots of human nature, a man of the new school of thought who could demonstrate his theorem by the new 'method'.

To the hostile majority he appeared a man of intolerable conceit. That is the note so constantly struck. Who is this individual, they say, this 'Malmesburiense animal'? He sets himself alone against the wisdom of the ages; against Aristotle; against the majestic precedents of the Law; against the bishops; against the presbyters — the right-thinking majority of able, conventional men. One can imagine what notoriety these startling doctrines must have obtained, in particular among young minds hostile to cant and humbug. And he added insult to injury by calmly suggesting that the book should be taught in the Universities. Hobbes was certainly a pig-headed and dogmatic old Wiltshireman: but for all his alleged timidity, he can hardly be accused of cowardice.

Such were the steps which led up to the launching of this cumulative attack. But before examining the counter-offensive it provoked, it is worth noting the sequel for Hobbes.

He had another card up his sleeve. During his exile, while consorting with the philosophers and mathematicians of Paris, with Gassendi and Mersenne, he had developed his materialist attack on the old metaphysical outlook. Having set out a revolutionary theory of the state, he now turned his attention to the philosophers.

The deterministic materialism of the *Elements of Philosophy* was launched on the world in 1655. Its un-compromising support of the doctrine of Necessity as

53

opposed to Free Will landed Hobbes into a hoary old controversy, with vivid theological implications. It particularly enraged the Churchmen — naturally enough. The more so, as the year before there had appeared a pirated edition of a paper privately written by Hobbes in debate with Bishop Bramhall during his exile. It was called *Of Liberty and Necessity*. In 1655 the indignant Bramhall seized the opportunity to publish his own reply, so Hobbes took up the cudgels in the next year. The Anglicans, seasoned in controversy with the Calvinists, argued for Free Will. The sequel was Bramhall's *Castigation* and the *Catching of the Leviathan*, published in 1658. Meanwhile, besides theological critics not here examined, Hobbes already had Filmer, Rosse, Seth Ward, Lucy and Lawson on his track.

Not content with this imbroglio, the old man — now getting on for seventy — must needs take on the Professors of Astronomy and Geometry at Oxford on their own ground. This academic mare's-nest was the most violent of all his controveries. He had claimed to square the circle, and Dr. Wallis's *Due correction for Mr. Hobbes, or School Discipline for not saying his Lessons right* set the tone for a personal vendetta. Aspersions were cast on Hobbes' loyalty, and in 1662 he wrote *Considerations on the Reputation Loyalty, Manners and Religion of Mr. Hobbes*, a ferocious self justification.[1]

He was still to write (*c.* 1668) *Behemoth, Four Dialogues on the Civil Wars*. It remained unpublished until after his death. The outlook is strongly anti-Parliamentarian, and the book was calculated to make the maximum of mis-

---

[1] See Collected Works, vol. IV, pp. 413-40.

chief in the context of its time. Hobbes further engaged in other minor controversies, and set about translating the Iliad and Odyssey, 'because there is nothing else for me to do'. He died, in the full tide of disputation, at the age of ninety-one.[1]

Such, in broad outline, was the development of Hobbes' attack, and such the sequence of his impact on his contemporaries. These rather obvious landmarks are worth recapitulating: they define the target at which his critics were directing their counter-attack.

But the main outline of Hobbes' doctrines is familiar. In spite of the scholastic flavour of much of his thought, Hobbes' outlook was typical of his age, both in his mechanical rationalism, and in his confidence in systematic method, though he was a much more thoroughgoing materialist than his contemporaries.

He is a prophet of a cynical, deterministic and utilitarian political theory, which discards the old sanctions of natural reason reflecting a Divine order, and which replaces it by the imposition of arbitrary power as the price of security. He repudiates the alternative — the standard by which government, as distinct from society, is to be judged. He attempts to destroy the concepts both of a constitutional frame of society superior to executive government and of a cosmic order superior to man-made institutions. In his conception of sovereignty, which owed much to Bodin, though it implicitly repudiates Bodin's subjection of government to God, he was a

---

[1] Aubrey's life of Hobbes in its full text remains the most valuable account of Hobbes' personality. It is to be found in Clark's edition of the *Brief Lives*, and in Mr. Anthony Powell's modern selection. Further, a new light has been thrown on the relationship between Aubrey and Hobbes in Mr. Powell's admirable *John Aubrey and his Friends*, Eyre & Spottiswode (London, 1949).

pioneer in his age, and by advocating the subordination of religion to political authority and by his dislike of corporations within the commonwealth, he paved the way for modern utilitarianism, concepts of positive law and of concentrated state power.

In his *Early Institutions* the great Victorian legist, Sir Henry Maine, makes a famous analysis of the origins and limitations of the Austinian conception of sovereignty. 'As far as my knowledge extends', he wrote, 'I do not think that any material portion of it is older than Hobbes,' who first defined it 'with a keenness of intuition and lucidity of statement which have never been rivalled'.[1] Hobbes, he says, discerned the outstanding fact of his time, the rise of centralized state power. The old multiform feudal and rural society was going down, and his theory reflects a new, urban order: 'We have heard of a village Hampden, but a village Hobbes is inconceivable.' The 'stored up force of society' was now to be wielded with increasing efficiency. Yet, Maine concludes, the very originality of Hobbes' conceptions threw him off balance, made his analysis too abstract. He and his Benthamite and Austinian followers cast aside the distinction between government and society, and disregarded the fact of the normal conditioning of power by the great body of custom, habit, opinion and institutions which have their roots in a primitive past, of which Hobbes was wholly ignorant.

[1] SIR HENRY MAINE, *Lectures on the Early History of Institutions* (seventh edition), John Murray (London, 1914), pp. 354-5.

CHAPTER III

SIR ROBERT FILMER; ALEXANDER ROSSE

IF one turns from the sceptical and materialistic rationalism of Hobbes to the traditional outlook of Filmer and of Rosse, the change in atmosphere and assumptions is remarkable. Filmer's attack is bound up with his criticism of Milton on Salmasius, and of Grotius's *De Jure Belli ac Pacis*.[1] He opens by attacking Hobbes' main argument that the law of nature is self-preservation. In a state of nature, says Hobbes, there is 'a liberty for each man to use his own power as he wills . . . for the preservation of his own life'. But this state of anarchy, argues Filmer, is incompatible with the authority given to Adam at the creation. For God gave Adam 'not only the dominion over the woman, and the children that should issue from them, but also over the whole earth to subdue it, so that, as long as Adam lived, no man could claime or enjoy anything but by Donation, Assignment, or Permission from him'. It follows that the lawless state of nature Hobbes imagines never existed. And as for his argument that such a state of nature may be going on in America, even Hobbes admits 'a government there of families'. But the mere fact of such a government, 'how small or brutish soever', is 'sufficient to destroy his *jus naturae*'.

Far from the state of universal violence and fear being

[1] *Observations concerning the Originall of Government, upon Mr. Hobs' Leviathan, Mr. Milton against Salmasius, (and) H. Grotius De Jure Belli* (London, 1652).

the law of life, Filmer maintains that the law of self-preservation, so much stressed by Hobbes, demands peace. 'For the Law of Nature and the Right of Nature are one, and the Law of nature is a command to preserve life . . . not to destroy it.'

Hobbes, moreover, says Filmer, following his artificial and erroneous assumptions, argues that no one will be the first to lay down his natural rights. Other men will consequently maintain theirs. This assumption, Filmer insists, if it were true, would postpone indefinitely the creation of a Commonwealth, 'though all men should spende their whole lives in nothing else than running up and down to covenant'. Further, the state of pristine anarchy implies that men must have 'sprung up like mushrooms [*fungorum more*] all together'. If Hobbes' picture of the origin of society were valid, no Commonwealth would ever have been realized. As to his idea of men abdicating the power of resistance when setting up an artificial 'Leviathan', it is against his own version of the law of self-preservation. 'For if right of nature be a liberty to use power for the preservation of life, laying down that power must be a relinquishing of power to preserve or defend life.' At the end of the transaction the individual is helpless, at the mercy of government. He has violated Hobbes' basic Law of Nature, the right to preserve his own security.

Even if Hobbes regarded his original contract as a fiction,[1] this argument is ingenious and difficult to answer. The absolutism of the *Leviathan* and the revolutionary conditions which it would have probably provoked must ultimately tend to misgovernment and insecurity.

[1] 'We must notice that Hobbes' argument does not require that his state of nature ever historically existed. It is an abstraction; it is what would happen if at any moment the sovereign power was removed.' A. D. LINDSAY, op. cit., p. xxi.

Far from such a government being efficient, it would break down, and the whole laborious contrivance collapse. Filmer, it would seem, has here pointed out one fundamental flaw in the argument, touched on in a very different context by a modern critic of Hobbes.[1]

Such argument, says Filmer, can lead only to anarchy. Hobbes presents the people 'with a very large commission of array' in a war of all against all. And for his assertion that the absence of civil government implies a perpetual state of war, there is no evidence. Only in abnormal conditions of famine would such a situation come about. 'Indeed if such a multitude of men should be created as the earth could not well nourish, there might be cause for men to destroy one another, rather than perish for want of food.' But the earth is not so overpopulated, nor the environment of mankind so harsh. 'God,' says Filmer, with all the confidence of a seventeenth-century Englishman, 'was no such niggard at the creation.' It follows that one of Hobbes' main arguments falls to the ground. The natural condition of man is not one of perpetual war.

'So there is no absolute necessity of warre in a state of pure nature.' On the contrary, if self-preservation is man's main end, it is the duty of every man to live in peace 'that so he may tend to the preservation of his life, which, while he is in actual warre, he cannot do'.

Filmer then proceeds to criticize Hobbes' constitutional ideas. It is untrue to pretend that by some magic the 'plurality' of wills in Hobbes' assembly are 'reduced

---

[1] See PLAMENATZ, op. cit., p. 16: 'Bentham and the Utilitarians, for instance, are as certain as Hobbes that men ought not to trust one another. But they happened to be more afraid of misgovernment than anarchy. They therefore argued that because men are selfish, vain, and naturally abusive of power, only a democratic government can secure them against each other's ill usage.'

to one will'. 'To reduce all the wills of one assembly by plurality of voices to one will,' he argues, 'is not a proper speech, for it is not a plurality but a totality of voices that maketh an assembly of one will.' Unless you have totality, all that will be obtained is a 'majority vote — the will of a major part of the assembly'. Filmer is also critical of the idea of a 'Representative'. If it be 'democraticall', if all the people make a mutual covenant, who is there left over to rule? And if there is a 'Representative aristocrati-call', 'free from covenanting' they are irresponsible and can cut each other's throats. In this case, Hobbes' arguments could only lead to monarchy: in 'this his moulding of a multitude into one person in the generation of his great Leviathan, the King of the children of Pride' — a fine phrase. Hobbes is cheating by his argument that an artificial state resolves the problem of divergent wills. Moreover, says Filmer, the whole edifice of the Leviathan is undermined by Hobbes allowing so wide a right of resistance.

' 'These last doctrines are destructive of all Government whatsoever and even to the Leviathan itself. Hereby any rogue or villain may murder his sovereign, if the sovereign but offer by force to whip or lay him in the stocks, since whipping may be said to be a wounding, and putting in the stocks an imprisonment.' Hobbes' society would thus combine tyranny with anarchy. It is impracticable and morally pernicious. Further, says Filmer, in his preface, the very title is misleading. 'I wish the title of the book had not been of a Commonwealth, but of a weale Publique, or Common-weale, which is the true word carefully observed by the translator of Bodin "de Republica" into English: many ignorant men are apt by the name of

Commonwealth to understand a popular Government, wherein wealth and all things shall be common, tending to the levelling of the community to the state of pure nature.' Hobbes has, therefore, been doubly misleading, even in his title.

Although Filmer, as he admitted in his preface, had read 'Mr. Hobs' book', 'with no small content', his objection to Hobbes' 'Means of acquiring' sovereignty was radical. Only by a patriarchal authority, sanctioned by an unchanging moral order, can sovereign power be justified, for it is in nature arbitrary. To Filmer the attempt to base a utilitarian power on will seemed profoundly unsatisfactory and based on a misreading of the laws of nature.

These rather sparse and limited but sometimes telling arguments Filmer, in a short pamphlet, brought to bear on Hobbes.

A more thorough, if more academic, critic must now be considered.

II

Some account of Alexander Rosse has already been given; of the popularity and extent of his numerous and curious works; of his writing six volumes of a continuation of Sir Walter Raleigh's History of the world, of his attempt to confute Sir Thomas Browne on 'Vulgar Errors', and of his attack on Hobbes.

The copy of his *Leviathan Drawn out with a Hook: or Animadversions on Mr. Hobbs his Leviathan* now in the Codrington Library at All Souls College, Oxford, runs to 102 pages of small print.[1] It is an affair of old-fashioned scholastic learning; the work of an elderly, benevolent and judicious man, anxious not to be drawn into a personal vendetta with Hobbes, but determined to do his best to prevent the *Leviathan* from doing harm.

The dedication to Francis Lucy concludes, 'The Ichneumon is but a small rat, yet it can kill the great crocodile. There is more nourishment in the small lark than in the kite or raven, — As in a little bee, so in this little book there is much spirit.' He refers to Francis Lucy's 'hopeful son, my scholar'. The whole tone is intimate and genial, very different from the fierce rationalistic atmosphere of Hobbes' mind. Rosse then proceeds to the Preface, stating the purpose of the book.

'Being desired by some of my friends a while ago to peruse Mr. *Hobbs* his *Leviathan*, and deliver my opinion of it. I have done accordingly, I finde him a man of excellent parts and in this book much gold, and withal much dross. He hath mingled his wine with too much water and embittered his pottage with too much Coloquintida. There are some of his positions which may prove of dangerous consequence, to green heads . . . under green grass lurk oftentimes snakes and serpents, such as *Euri-*

---

[1] It belonged to Codrington himself, an indication that Rosse was still read in the eighteenth century. In this copy the following Latin inscription is written:
In Doctissimum Marinae belluae domitorem, Al. Rosseum.
('On the most learned tamer of the marine monster' — Al. Rosse.)
    Alcides clava Lernaeum perculit hydram,
    Sed tu, Ros, calamo, monstra marina domas.
    Quantum Leviathan superavit viribus Hydram;
    Tantum, Ros, superas Amphytrioniadem.
This is English'd in the text thus:
    Hercles his club did Lernæa's Hydra kill,
    But thow, Ross, quell'st sea monsters with thy quill.
    How much Leviathan exceeded Hydra,
    As much, Rosse, thow beat'st Hercles Amphytrionida.

dice perceived not, till they be stung to death. I have, therefore (not to wrong Mr. *Hobbes* but to vindicate the truth, for *in Republica libera oportet linguas esse liberas*) adventured upon his *Leviathan*.'

The Monster, he says, is after all not so terrible. 'It can be drawn out with a Hook.' He aims rather 'at verity, than victory', though Hobbes slights learned men and 'prideth himself too much in his scales'.

There follows an address to the Reader, rather in the manner of Sir Thomas Browne. The *Leviathan*, Rosse argues, is blasphemous. Here Rosse mentions various theological heresies, most important to him. It says that 'covetousness and ambition and injustice with power are honorable; that tyrants and good Princes are all one; . . . that Princes are not subject to their own laws; that private men have no property in their goods. That it was a winde and not the Holy Spirit which in the Creation moved on the waters; that Christ hath no spiritual Kingdom here on earth; that He did not cast out devils, but onely cured madness. Such, and much more like stuff and smoke, doth this Leviathan send out of his nostrils. This is the spermacaetae or spawn which the whale casteth out . . . a whale that hath vomited up the condemned opinion of the hereticks, and chiefly the Anthropomorphits, Sabellians, Nestorians, Saduceans, Arabeans, Tacians or Eucratits, Manichies, Mahumetans, and others; for in holding life eternal to be only on earth, he is a Cerinthian and a Mahumetan; in giving God corporeity he is an Anthropomorphit, a Manichean, a Tertullianist and an Andean: in holding the Three Persons to be distinct names and essences . . . he is a Sabellian, a Montanist, an Aetian, and a Priscillianist. In saying that Christ personated God the

Son, he is a Nestorian, giving him two personalities, and in denying spirits he is a Saducean: in making the soul to rest with the body till the resurrection he is an Arabian; in making the soul of man corporal he is a Luciferian, by putting a period to Hell he is an Origenist: in teaching dissimulation in religion he is a Tacian or Eucratit, in making God the cause of injustice or sin he is a Manichee; in slighting Christ's miracles he is a Jew; and in making our natural reason the word of God he is a Socinian.' Yet, he concludes, after this catalogue of iniquity, 'I quarrel not with Mr. Hobbs, but with his book, which not onely I, but many more, who are both learned, and judicious, men, look upon as a piece dangerous both to Government and Religion'.

Such is the case opened against Hobbes. Rosse is concerned primarily with the religious implications of Hobbes' doctrines. And he denies their originality. Here is nothing, he says, but old and pernicious heresy. For Hobbes is a Manichee.

The accusation of Manichaeanism is fundamental. Hobbes, Rosse argues, was blaspheming life: he attributes radical evil to human nature. By denying the capacity of Reason to apprehend God, and confining it within the rigid pattern of causation, he is simply reviving an ancient and familiar dualism. Hobbes regards himself as cut off from the direct apprehension of Deity, 'from the first power of all powers, the first cause of all causes'. Having made this formidable point, which puts the *Leviathan* in a new and damaging perspective, Rosse proceeds to his full theme. He systematically traverses Hobbes' text, point by point. And, with the main text, comes the detailed attack.

To take some of the main points in order. He first criticizes Hobbes' fundamental doctrine of motion. 'Life', says Hobbes, 'is but the motion of limbs.' But life, argues Rosse, is not motion, rather its cause. There may be life in limbs when there is no motion, as in sleep, or in 'hysterical women' (presumably in hysterical paralysis). On the other hand, there is motion without life, 'as in a wooden leg'.

Here is an inadequate but justified attempt to deal with Hobbes' basic assumption. Rosse further attacks his criticism of the orthodox schools of learning. As a scholar, he says, Hobbes here 'fouls his own nest' and shows presumption. 'Nor shall Aristotle, Plato, Cicero, Thomas, or other eminent men fear that Hobbes' whimsies and dreams thrust their solid and grave learning out of doors.' His criticism of Hobbes' doctrine of Felicity, the end of man's endeavour and the object of the State, is more fundamental.

'Felicity', Hobbes maintains, 'is a continual progress of desire.' But such a condition is impossible in this life; 'In Heaven is only true Felicity, because St. Austin saith we shall desire nothing that is absent,' a typical medieval debating point. Even Hobbes 'saith "the felicity of beasts consists in enjoying their quotidian food" '. It is the enjoying, insists Rosse, that counts: that is where the felicity comes in. Not the desire for food, which can be painful. Felicity, in fact, means 'fulfilment'. And as to Hobbes' theory that all men are equal by nature, that is clean contrary to truth. Equal they are in essential 'perfection of soul, but in accidental perfections we find the contrary'. Some, Rosse argues, for example, are 'dumb, blind, etc., dull, foolish, stupid; nay, there is naturally selection among beasts. To say there is no inequality in nature, is to say there is no order in nature'. After these fundamental points, he attacks the main political theme. 'Covenants are but words and breath', says Hobbes. But consent 'is an act of the soul and words uttered are symbols of the mind . . . There be also many mental and implicite or tacite covenants made without words. Abraham and Noah had been but in a bad condition if the covenants that God made with them had been but words and breath'.

Rosse next attacks a basic argument of Hobbes' political theory. 'Whatsoever a prince doth,' he says, 'can be no injury to the subject.' 'This doctrine will hardly down with freeborn people who choose to themselves princes, not to tyrannize over them but to rule them.' The people were 'not so mad as to think . . . that Tyrants must not be accused of injustice, for although the prince acteth by the people's authority in things lawful, yet in his lawless exorbitances he acteth of his own tyrannizing power'. Here is the medieval concept of a prince as only part of a commonwealth. To regard him otherwise is to confuse despotic and paternal dominion. 'This is to put no difference between the father and the butcher of his country. A King governs and is governed by Lawes — a Tyrant hath no Law but his will.' Here Rosse is in the old medieval tradition going back to Isidore of Seville and John of Salisbury, to Bracton and Fortescue: similar arguments are used by Hunton, Lawson and Whitehall.

He then proceeds to confute Hobbes' statement, 'that whether a Commonwealth be monarchical or popular, the freedom is still the same.' 'This I deny, for in an absolute

monarchy there is no liberty, but mere slavery, which is
the condition of those who live under the Turks, the
Muscovite, Prester John and the Magol.'

Further, says Hobbes, in analysing 'diseases of commonwealth', it is wrong to put conscience before obedience. But, counters Rosse, 'it is the curb of conscience
that restrains men from rebellion: there is no outward
Law or force so powerful ... There is no judge so severe,
no Torturer so cruel, as an accusing conscience. This
Saul, Judas, Orestes, and so many more knew, who would
rather be their own executioners ... than be tormented
by the firebrands of those snakey-haired furies whose
residence is an evil conscience'. The foundations of political order must be found in men's hearts. Moreover,
Hobbes will not even have the sovereign subject to his
own Laws. 'What availeth Alexander to conquer the
world', asks Rosse, arguing in the old moralizing traditional way, 'and not conquer himself?' As Aristotle tells
us, 'the Law where it is plain and perspicuous, ought to
bear Rule, because without it no King or Commonwealth
can govern. No Commonwealth can be happy or continue
long, but where the Prince is as well subject to the Law
as the people'. Here is the old classical and medieval
subjection of politics to morals, the basis of traditional
political thought. The council of Pittacus, says Rosse,
was good; 'Let him not break the Law that made the
Law' — *Pareto legi quisquis legem sanxerit.*[1]

Hobbes, on the other hand, implies that 'unjust actions
joined with power are honourable'. But, says Rosse,
echoing St. Augustine, 'Where there is government, unjust actions are punished, not honored, and if it were not

[1] Pittacus, *c.* 688-570 B.C. Lawgiver and ruler of Mitylene in Lesbos.

so, Kingdoms would be nothing else but dens of theeves. *Remota justitia, quid aliud sunt regna quam magna latrocinia?*' 'Honour doth not meerly consist in the opinion of power. By this means Mr. Hobbes may maintain that honour is due to Garlick, Onions, Crocodiles, Dogs, Cats, because the Egyptians worshipped them.' Power is only justified if it is moral.

Hobbes is also unsound on the question of property. He attacks those who say that 'every private man hath a property in his goods'. 'Among the Turks, indeed,' says Rosse, 'no private man hath any property at all. But, under Christian Princes private men live more happily.' Here, to be repeated by later critics, was one of the most damaging of Rosse's allegations.

Turning then to more theological speculation, Rosse argues that Hobbes is wrong when he says that the Spirit of God, moving upon the face of the waters, meant a wind. On the contrary, it was a Spirit; and for Hobbes to say that the term ghost is a figment of the brain is to pervert the truth. 'For it signifieth a real immaterial substance, which we call from the Latin word, Spirit, and so it was always used by the Saxons, and to this day "*gheest*" and "*gheist*" in Low Dutch do signify the same thing.'

After this telling, and to him important, point, Rosse's peroration begins.

Hobbes dislikes Aristotle, he says, for the philosopher stands in the way of his own works being read in Universities. 'Aristotle's brightness doth so dazzle his weak sight that he cannot be seen in the colleges. I know Apes and Crows think their own breed fairest. Who, then, can blame Mr. Hobbes for having so good a conceit of his Leviathan? It will not be an easy matter for Mr. Hobbes to jostle Aristotle out of the Universities, nor to make Malmesbury as famous as Stagira . . . Shall the beetle thrust the eagle out of his nest?'

'I think', he concludes, 'the path of one Elias a Jew will be fitter for him. He writes that Leviathan is a great fish laid up long since in pickle, to be food for the just in the Kingdom of Messias here on earth. Mr. Hobbes expecteth such a Kingdom: therefore I think he cannot employ his Leviathan better, than to salt it against that day.'

There is, indeed, nothing else to do with it, for Hobbes' subversive arguments are not likely to get the book accepted in Universities. Rosse feels so strongly about the matter that he falls into two pages of Latin quotation. He quotes Scaliger, Carden (de Subtil: *Plurimum interest reipublicae ut Aristoteles conservetur*), Melanchthon, Erasmus, Keckermanus, Zanchius and Casaubon.

'Mr. Hobbes doth struggle not only against Aristotle, but against the most eminent men of all times. Therefore, I have alleged the chief learned of the Protestants, to justify the Prince of Philosophers. Scaliger calls Aristotle the incomparable hero of learning, and the divine eagle of knowledge. Carden saith that he excelled in all learning, with incredible sagacity without any conspicuous error. Melanchthon said that Aristotle is so needful for a Commonwealth that he should be carefully preserved and read in schools and universities, for without him no learning nor method can be had. Erasmus acknowledges him to be the Prince and Perfection of Philosophy, and laments that the greatest parts of his works are lost. Keckerman calls him the miracle of nature. P. Martyr sheweth that Aristotle's pains were profitable. Zanchie

saith that he is of all philosophers the most excellent;
Casaubon calls him with admiration, a "man of men",
whose style is fraught with Attic eloquence . . . and
declares, "that they who write or speak against him are
dunces, and such whose books are fit for nothing but
the fire". Scaliger calls such barbarous wits, Rats, Kites,
Crows, Ravens, Owls and Bats.'

'To conclude,' said Rosse, rather surprisingly, 'I would
have Mr. Hobbes take notice that I have no quarrel
against him, but against his tenets.'

Such are the main points and such the idiom and atmosphere of Rosse's argument. What is the significance of
the attack? In the political aspect Rosse brings the
fundamental assumptions of the ancient classical and
medieval tradition to bear on Hobbes' new-fangled
justification of naked power. Power, he maintains, is
conditional. 'What availeth Alexander to conquer the
world, and not to conquer himself?' *Pareto Legi quisquis legem sanxerit.* Rosse's admirable phrases state the
truth well. Such constitutionalism had a great tradition
behind it; and it was to have a great future. The rule
of Law has been proved in practice a foundation of stable
government; Rosse insists on it from the moral and
theological aspect. We may add (taking a leaf out of
Hobbes' own book) the proven fact that such government
has proved highly successful.

Further, Rosse maintains, Hobbes' ideas are not
fundamentally new. This point of view, with its denial
of the capacity of the human mind on its own level to
apprehend the order of the universe; with its blasphemy
of life, its reduction of society to something organized
apart from God — what is it but the old Manichaean

heresy, familiar to St. Augustine? What is it but the pagan attempt to be self-sufficient, the anthropocentric arrogance which can end only in catastrophe? In view of the present perils of mankind, there will be many who will regard Rosse's re-statement of the old outlook as worth consideration.

CHAPTER IV

DR. SETH WARD; THE REVEREND WILLIAM LUCY'S *OBSERVATIONS*

A YEAR after the appearance of Rosse's attack on Hobbes the counter-offensive was reinforced by a young man of very different background. The context of Dr. Seth Ward's pamphlet defending the Universities against Hobbes' threat to intellectual freedom has already been described. Ward was writing not primarily as a clergyman, but as a scientist. Though he was afterwards to be eminent in the Church, it was in his capacity of Professor of Astronomy at Oxford that he took the initiative.

The other critic to be considered here was also destined to be a bishop. Dr. William Lucy is not a writer of high calibre, but he possesses a quaint sincerity and he is representative of average opinion. His *Observations* appeared in 1657. Writing under the name of 'William Pike, Christophilus', the future Bishop of St. Davids develops a rather ordinary argument. But it is probably a good deal more typical of the reaction of the majority of the clergy than the high-powered rhetoric of Rosse and the brilliant invective of Bramhall.

II

Seth Ward's contribution was short but effective. The appendix to *Vindiciae Academiarum* (1654) covers ten pages, and considers only one aspect of Hobbes — 'What

72

WARD; LUCY'S 'OBSERVATIONS'

he hath spoken of the Universities in his *Leviathan*.'
Ward's other and major criticism was philosophical: it
does not directly concern his political views and it is outside the range of the present enquiry.

Within limits, Ward's defence of intellectual freedom
is clear and sound. What, he asks, is Hobbes' end? What
his means? What his expectation or prospect of success?
Quoting the well-known passage in which Hobbes
blandly hopes that a powerful prince will one day translate
his device into reality, Ward remarks that the end he
proposes is for the world to 'be regulated exactly by that
modell which he there exhibits, and that his reason should
be the governing reason of mankind'.

How is this objective to be brought about? By public
teaching in the Universities, enforced by 'entire sovereignty'. This project Ward thinks intolerable. 'Are not the
Universities of England,' he asks, 'learned enough already?'

'It will now concern us,' he continues, 'to consider his
expectation and hope, concerning the accomplishment of
this (sober and modest) designe.' This delusion must
reflect the advanced age of the old gentleman, when
'Jealousy and Spleen have prevailed over him'. Further,
Hobbes' basic ideas are taken from theories already current in the Universities. For example, his fundamental
argument that sense is but a perception of motion. The
'theory of explaining sence upon the grounds of motion,
was almost generally received here before his Booke came
forth. Being sufficiently taught by Des Cartes, Gassendus,
Sir K[enelm] Digby . . .' It has, actually, been put forward precisely in this form 'in Mr. Warners' Papers . . . on
vision'. Here, as one would expect, Ward is up to date and
differs from Rosse, with his more old-fashioned outlook.

73

Hobbes' attack on the Universities because of their scholastic origins particularly exasperates the professor of Astronomy. 'In truth, Sir, I hardly know how to behave myself upon this occasion.'

The whole case, Ward insists, is ridiculous. Hobbes' views are hopelessly out of date. He identifies the Anglican Universities, which have been remodelled 'by commission from the Civill Power', with Popish institutions. 'This whole discourse is freakish, and unbecoming the Archipoliticall gravity of a Master of the world.' As for his frivolous remarks on 'Fayries' to the disparagement of religion, they can best be answered in their own coin. 'Well sir,' says Ward, 'since he will have his frollick, I am resolved to answer this passage with a Crochet of a Friend of mine, whose observation is that however the *Fayries* are said to be harmelesse in their dancings he is sure the Hobbe-goblins are spightfull and mischeivous in their Friskings.'

The Universities, of course, do not now hold the crazy opinions Hobbes attributes to them: they have long rejected scholasticism. He complains of the 'insignificant language' of the schoolmen and cites the commentaries of Peter Lombard — an utterly irrelevant argument in the middle of the seventeenth century. 'What is the language of *Peter Lombard* . . . to the Universities of *Oxford* or *Cambridge?*' Only in the moon would such propositions now be maintained. Perhaps, indeed, when Hobbes was up at Magdalen Hall years ago, such jargon was in the air. Today the atmosphere is very different, says the confident young Wadham don of twenty-eight.

And Hobbes has absolutely no business to attack the Universities on scientific or geometrical grounds. 'I dare undertake him not to be so great a Geometrician as he pretends to be.'

In conclusion, Ward returns to his main attack. Hobbes, he says, is trying to destroy freedom of thought. What pains him is the desire that 'Aristotelity may be changed into Hobbeity, & instead of the Stagyrite, the world may adore the great Malmesburian Phylosopher'. It is, above all, unpardonable that Hobbes should attempt to have his ideas 'imposed by a magistrate'.

The Savilian Professor had delivered a telling criticism of one of the most dangerous of Hobbes' arguments, and in a short space contributed notably to the general counter-attack. It differs in kind from that of Filmer and Rosse. Both had expressed a thoroughly traditional point of view; to them Hobbes is an innovator, when he is not a heretic. Seth Ward, a younger man, concentrating on a more limited aspect of Hobbes, regards him as hopelessly old fashioned. The older generation, brought up in the old learning, found Hobbes' views intolerable: the young, representative of seventeenth-century science thought them grotesque. The *Leviathan*, in his view, advocated an intellectual tyranny as formidable as the reign of Aristotelian scholasticism from which Ward's generation had but recently escaped. Hobbes would have checked the free development of speculation — a freedom, as Ward realized, which was to make their century one of the most creative in history.

I I I

Bishop Lucy's book opens with a weighty dedication to William Seymour, first Marquis of Hertford and second Duke of Somerset, and it is worth recapitulating the career of this generous patron of learning.[1] Born in 1588, the great-grandson of Protector Somerset, he was one of the outstanding public characters of his day and played a distinguished part in the Civil War. Educated at Magdalen College, Oxford, he was twice Chancellor of the University. When an undergraduate he is said to have been the lover of Lady Arabella Stuart, who was then living at Woodstock. In 1610 they were secretly married and both attempted to escape to the Low Countries. After a series of dramatic vicissitudes, Lady Arabella was apprehended on shipboard, and again incarcerated in the Tower. On her death, her lover returned to England, and in 1618 married Lady Frances Devereux, eldest daughter of the second Earl of Essex. In the Civil War the King appointed him to the command of the western counties, and he was left in charge of the Royalist garrison at Oxford after Charles's flight into East Anglia. At the King's execution, it was Hertford who begged permission to take the body to Windsor for burial. He had been governor to Prince Charles, though the charge, according to Clarendon was 'contrary to his normal constitution', which after a wild youth was such that he 'loved his book above all exercises'. He possessed extensive property in Wiltshire, principally at Savernake, where he was the owner of a great estate centring on Tottenham House and hereditary Warden of the Forest.[2] He also had property at Netley, to which, during the Interregnum, he was confined. He was

---

[1] *Observations, Censures and Confutations of Diverse Errors in the* 12th, 13th and 14th *Chapters of Mr. Hobbs his Leviathan* (1657).

[2] See THE EARL OF CARDIGAN, *The Wardens of Savernake Forest*, Routledge & Kegan Paul (London, 1949), pp. 175-87.

re-created Duke of Somerset in 1660, in which year he died. Hertford, says Lucy, cannot avoid being patron of his book. 'I boldy say (perhaps unmannerly), that I make you patron of it and whether you like it or no.' For here, in Hertford's person, is the living refutation of Hobbes' 'villainous aspersions on the human nature'. I shall answer Hobbes, says Lucy, thus. 'See, here an Heroique person who hath found a Rock to bottome his Religion upon.' When Hobbes discourses of the full equality of man by nature, here is the Marquess of Hertford, the living refutation of such nonsense. 'I can', says the obsequious clergyman, 'produce your Lordship . . .'

There is nothing, he says, ordinary in Hertford. He is 'composed for greatness, differing even in naturall disposition as much from other men as a Lion from other beasts'. Lord Hertford, he insists, needs no external law to guide him — 'to afright or perswade'. He has a Law within his soul, he is a 'son of Nature'. Thus, he continues, 'I shall confute that universal baseness hee [Hobbes] attributes to Mankind'.

It follows that Hertford must be patron to the book — and since he is thus committed, he may as well read it. 'Let it receive a cast of your eye and a roome in your Study; for the Author hee is a man loves darkness and quiet.' He is not, of course, after patronage, and for that matter, he does not fear frowns. He simply dedicates the book to his Lordship out of admiration.

It is useless to pretend that the Reverend William Lucy possessed an intellect of high calibre. Rather, he gives the impression of a well meaning, rather flustered old gentleman, not well able to keep up with events. The preface to the reader strikes a querulous note, as well it might. When at last, at the Restoration, he got his Bishopric, it was to be St. Davids.

He has, he insists, been much put upon. His complaint, already quoted, is also worth recalling: 'My Study abid the fate of better libraries, and was rifled in those unhappie times of warre when to have anything was a crime . . .' That last phrase has a touch of uncomprehending exasperation. It was natural enough. He had suffered sequestration in the turbulent years when the book was written: the murder of his patron, Buckingham, may have left its mark on him young.

It is idle to pretend, moreover, that the opening part of the book is an outstanding contribution to thought, though the titles in his elaborate contents table are promising. 'Eternity', for example, 'explained againe'; and 'A Digression to prove that there was no Idolatry before the Flood'.

After some metaphysical arguments about first causes, Lucy points an accusing and moralizing finger at Hobbes, and taxes him with ingratitude to his Creator. What will Hobbes say to God on the last day, when the Almighty will arraign him for abuse of his great gifts? 'I have assisted thee with the purchase of so much learning; how hast thou used it to mine honour?' Hobbes, says Lucy, in a good phrase, 'has spent his life studying to countenance atheistical wits with shows of reason for their wickedness'. The old sinner only believes what he can see. When the reader meets with such 'muddy souled' writers, he should recall the words of Christ: 'Blessed are they that do not see and yet believe.'

This does not sound very original. It represents the answer of revealed religion, and Lucy expressed what the vast majority of men in his age believed to be the truth. But this study is primarily concerned with political criticisms of Hobbes. Lucy's rather tedious argument, with its scholastic flavour, that religion is a sort of justice because it gives God his due, but an imperfect justice since obviously man cannot give God his full due, may be passed over. He labours to confute Hobbes' opinion that religion is based on fear, 'till I come to his Treatise of Angels, which will administer occasion for further censure'. It is better worth turning to his seventh chapter, on the Natural Condition of Mankind. Hobbes, he says, 'makes man little better than an incarnate devil ... I will therefore for the honour of mankind, endeavour to rescue it from such foule scandals and aspersions'. This was a usual and justifiable view of Hobbes among his contemporaries. Although he has since been represented as a profound philosopher, concerned with an Olympian sadness about the 'human predicament' and yearning for a transitory felicity, it is likely that the contemporary view has something to be said for it in view of the implications of Hobbes' political thought. Hobbes, says Lucy, is an old scoundrel. He imputes a systematic wickedness to mankind.

Lucy may have been right. But his method of argument is not now very convincing, being bound up with jejune and obvious Biblical examples. 'Adam and Eve', he remarks, 'wished well to one another.' Mankind is not 'terrigena, borne out of the earth': 'the poore infant confides and trusts in his parents'. And how can one assume such a universal and calculated malignity in view of family affection? A child may wish to emulate his father, but this ambition does not imply hostility. Animals have family feeling, and to depict mankind as in a war of all against all is to make them 'more barbarous and beastly than the Beasts themselves'. Applying his commonplace but sensible mind further, Lucy remarks on the innate inequalities of prudence and ability in men. One cannot, he insists, generalize about them. There are, indeed, moral monsters, but they are exceptional. 'To say that men universely deale so maliciously for delectation is a most unhappy assertion.'

On the contrary, man is a social animal, only happy in society, and Hobbes' war against all is an 'unheard of' doctrine. Men are never without law. There is a power divine which keeps all men from perpetrating crimes against the law which is 'writ in their hearts'. As for Hobbes' picture of the state of nature, it is against experience. 'Let us think', he says, 'of men by several wrecks cast upon an uninhabited coast, and let us think then whether they are at war with one another . . . They would succour one another, and this humanity is writ in every man's heart, in which such wicked principles as his have not blotted it out.'[1] 'Let us consider them', he continues, 'either planting near other men, or planting for their own profit.' Of course, they will co-operate; it is the only sensible course. Further, he continues, Hobbes insists that men go around armed and keep their doors locked. 'These two', says the elderly clergyman, in a charming phrase, 'might be spared in my particular, who do neither.' But this precaution is only taken because of a minority of drunkards and criminals.

[1] This problem is discussed in a more recent context by Professor Hancock in his *Politics in Pitcairn*. He examines what actually happened among the descendants of the mutineers from the *Bounty* and comes to conclusions which are nearer Hobbes' view than Lucy's. See also Eachard, below, pp. 141-2.

Lucy declares that, on the contrary, men are born with 'abilities to do one another good'. They are born into a commonwealth; they do not artificially contrive one. Here is a fundamental argument: there is a 'frame' of society which no government has the right to break. If it does, there is an alternative and ultimate power in the Commonwealth apart from the government. Every man is born a citizen of the world. Here Lucy re-echoes Graeco-Roman tradition, rather incongruous in a seventeenth-century setting, in the relative provincialism of English society. Further, he insists, primitive peoples do not live in anarchy. Even 'the Americans' are not merely brutish, but 'have justice executed amongst them for misdemeanours, as may appeare to any who reads their stories'.

As for Hobbes' comparison of kings and 'persons of Sovereigne Authority' in states to gladiators 'in a posture of warre', he thinks it 'very handsomly expressed and would willingly have let it alone' on this score, but, lest it should 'by the ingenuity of it steale a credit of his opinion with a Reader' he feels he must censure it. He does this with a pretty feeble argument. The armed sovereignty of States is a condition of preparedness for war, not war itself. They imagine each other to harbour aggressive designs. But that does not say all are aggressors all the time, and they are not permanently mobilized, 'drawne into the field'.[1]

After this rather weak point, Lucy attacks the part of Hobbes' doctrine he thinks most wicked of all, that Law is only the command of a superior, man-made, reflecting no cosmic sanction. Nothing in the state of nature can

[1] Chap. x, sect. 5.

be unjust, says Hobbes: 'where there is no common power, there is no Law'. This doctrine, Lucy insists, is radically subversive. It is 'Rubbidge'. 'Now I deny that there is nothing unjust to such men . . . the Law is that writ in their hearts . . . that Law of Nature, that Pratique Law.' And men know it by instinct. 'In the breach of such law there is horror and dread, insomuch as a man cannot live, for it is a prodigie to see a man without all Conscience.'[1]

There follows an historical passage in the consistently parochial idiom of Lucy's thought. 'Moses', he says, 'was the first that ever gave Laws to governe a nation by.' Those God-given laws were no innovation. The commandments were the expression of the Law of Nature, writ in men's hearts. 'I conceive the Decalogue to be like our Magna Charta. That was a brief and pithy expression of what was the old Law.' The seventeenth-century legend of Magna Charta as reflecting ancient Anglo-Saxon laws, so widely current, was well embedded in Lucy's mind. He also quotes an old point from Bracton, though he does not probably know its origin — the idea of *occupatio* whereby one 'begins a property'.[2]

'He who first gets possession is lord of the *bona utilia* of the world', the 'useful goods'. 'This is so in plantations, and when a man takes wild game.' 'But', he hastens to add, 'I speake not here of Deere, Conyes, Hares, nor Fishes in ponds, etc. which are impaled [fenced] . . .

---

[1] Chap. x, sect. 6. Compare A. D. LINDSAY (op. cit., p. xxii). 'Some kinds of moral behaviour are more elementary than government.' See also F. WATKINS, *The Political Tradition of the West*, chap. i, 'The Origins of Western Legalism' (O.U.P., for Harvard University Press, 1949); and PETER LASLETT, op. cit., on 'Patriarchalism'. Also my *Western Political Thought*, chap. i, on the need for emotional sanctions for conduct in a healthy commonwealth.

[2] See BRACTON, *De Legibus et Consuetudinibus Angliae*, III.

nor such things as our lawes, indulging the pleasure of
Gents and men of quality, have appropriated to certain
persons & places, as Pheasants . . . but whatsoever no
nationall particular Laws hath given to another, that the
law of nature gives to the first possessor; and this law
men find before any positive law of Nations in the
practice of the world.'[1] The Law of nature does not
encourage poaching.

He then turns to a curious argument. In the *De
Corpore Politico* Hobbes insisted that Natural Law is
unlimited self-preservation. This argument, says Lucy,
sets too much store by life. Many people have not set
such store by it, by their 'rotten House'. Death by some
is desired and 'wise-men have written much in contempt
of those sensual and temporall things, in which hee placeth
the only aime and happiness of man'. This world is
the mere gateway to the spiritual life, 'although perhaps
there may be some difficulties in opening the gate'.
Many pagans preferred death to dishonour; much more
do those who believe in immortality. They regard it
rather as a liberation, an increase of power. 'Who is
troubled to loose a bag of Silver, when in its roome
shall be left a bagge of gold?' 'It was said', he continues,
'of our Druids' (an early appearance), 'in England, who
taught the Immortality of the soule, it was a poor dull
thing to hang onto life. They would have said it was a
beastly thing if they had known, through the revelation
of Christ, that we do not lose by death'. The argument
is reinforced by maintaining that death itself is not
necessarily painful. 'Had he [Hobbes], been in a house
of mourning as I have, he would know that death is not

[1] Chap. x, sect. 10.

the worst evil. This gentleman, I guesse, hath onely looked upon death in those horrid vizards and disguises which fearful men mask it with.'

He proceeds to recount various pagan suicides and how the men of Antiquity set little store by life. And he tells a rather sad little story from his own experience, 'I can tell', he says, 'a story of a Child of mine owne, somewhat above foure years old, who being sickly, I put in a neighbour's house in whose care I confided to attend her, shee grew weaker and weaker unto death, & almost immediately before her death, the man of the house coming from his business, she called the woman whom she usually called "old Mother", "Old Mother," said she, "goe give the Old Man his breakfast, he wil be angry else, and leave such a boy to rock me in my Cradle", and so straightway died.'

If death had been painful, says the moralizing clergyman, the little girl would not have thought on such trivialities as the old man's breakfast. After this dialectical triumph, Lucy goes on to speak of old men 'who go out gently like candles', and who 'Drowse into what seems a sleep.' They are even annoyed at being wakened by 'the importunate hands of friends' — a point irrelevant to the feelings of those in the full tide of life.

He turns next to Hobbes' doctrine that all men by the Law of Nature have a right to all things — 'a good large commission'. Every man for himself, says Hobbes. 'To use the phrase of the time,' writes his critic, 'this gent is very selfish.' Not a bad comment on Hobbes.

For the core of the matter — whether there is a valid Natural Law preceding civil society — the future Bishop of St. Davids reserves his most daring argument. There must, he says, be a pre-existent Natural Law, or God would not have punished the inhabitants of Sodom in so signal a manner. They had attempted a most wicked and detestable assault upon two angels who were visiting Lot in disguise; and such was the demoralization of the city that this kind of conduct was quite usual. There can have been no law against it. If there had been, Lot, that upright man, would undoubtedly have had the law on them. Yet God was so angry that he razed those cities to the ground. How can this vengeance have been just if there was no Law for these men to violate? If there was no Law, 'why was God so Angry?' The people of Sodom, says Lucy, had 'smothered the light of Nature'. They were 'unnaturally' breaking a Natural law, independent and prior to, human edicts. Here, indeed, is a poser for Hobbes.

Such is the main sequence of Lucy's argument. It is not powerful, but it is vividly expressed; representative of decent average opinion. Conscience, co-operation, the Law of Nature 'writ in men's hearts'; 'planters' working together to subdue the wilderness — these ideas, with their transcendental sanction, were widespread. Active wickedness is the mark not of the majority of sensible men but of a minority of criminals. Man is a citizen of the world, and mankind are brothers. These ideas, much mocked by destructive political thinkers, have lately received remarkable reinforcement from modern psychology and anthropology. In spite of the political catastrophies of our age, we are, perhaps, less likely to write off Lucy as an old fool than the pseudo-Darwinian 'realists' of the nineteenth century.

CHAPTER V

A WHIG FORERUNNER, GEORGE LAWSON; THE SIGNIFICANCE OF PHILIP HUNTON

THE contributions of Sir Robert Filmer and Alexander Rosse, of Seth Ward and William Lucy, have now been examined. There remain six writers to be assessed, George Lawson and Philip Hunton; Archbishop Bramhall and Dr. Eachard; Lord Clarendon and John Whitehall.

The first two are constructive and important, forerunners of the Whig tradition.

The Reverend George Lawson, Rector of More in Shropshire, ably asserts the old ideas of Natural Law and Commonwealth. His *Examination of the political part of Mr. Hobbs his Leviathan* appeared in 1657, in the same year as Lucy's book. He is a very much abler man and he writes a businesslike prose. It will be recalled that he had almost completed, though not yet published, a large book called *Politica Sacra et Civilis*, on subjects treated of in *Leviathan*. There seems pretty conclusive evidence that Locke read it.[1]

Lawson is a formidable writer, with a knowledge of ecclesiastical and civil law, and an accurate grasp of Latin legal terms which he frequently employs. His

---

[1] From 1687 to 1689 Locke lived with a merchant Quaker at Rotterdam named Furley, the catalogue of whose library is extant. He possessed a copy of Lawson's book *Politica Sacra et Civilis*. It is also known that Locke had a copy himself, because his servant catalogued his books on his return to England, 1689. Locke was secretive about his reading: in 1706 he pretended not to have read certain of Hobbes' books in his possession. See Maclean, op. cit., *Cambridge Historical Review*, January 1947.

method is to select quotations from Hobbes and then insert his comments and argument. The first part of the book is concerned with politics;[1] the rest is mainly theological.[2] The argument runs parallel with that developed in his other work, *Politica Sacra et Civilis*, a much larger book of 455 pages arranged in sixteen alternate chapters, which examines civil and ecclesiastical power. It is also worth consideration, for it throws light on the attack on Hobbes.

In the *Examination* Lawson deals fully with 'the principal controversies of the times concerning the constitution of the State and Church of England [not Church and State], tending to Righteousness, Truth and Peace'.

He begins with an Epistle to the reader, which throws light on the composition of the other work. Here Lawson states that he had already finished the larger book, a thorough treatise on civil and ecclesiastical government which, 'if it had not been lost by some negligence after an Imprimatur was put upon it, might have prevented' the political part of the *Leviathan*. But in view of conditions in the censor's office in the mid-seventeenth century, Lawson had prudently retained another copy. 'Though one copy be lost, yet there is another, which may become publick hereafter.' The *Politica Sacra et Civilis* was, in fact, published in 1660, three years after the appearance of the criticism of the *Leviathan*.

Here, then, we have the closest link between the criticism of Hobbes and the Whig tradition. There is also a strong flavour of the Non-conformist conscience about

[1] pp. 1-147.   [2] pp. 148-214.

Lawson — particularly in the *Politica Sacra et Civilis*. A certain self-righteousness here becomes faintly tinged with cant. 'Thine, to serve in the Lord,' he says to the pious reader. The Civil Wars, he writes in the preface to this elaborate work, were a 'judgement' — a thought apt to emerge in England in face of catastrophe — leading to self-denial, and moral rearmament.

Moral rearmament was what Lawson preached. The wars were the result of our 'impenitency, prejudice, partiality, pride, obstinacy and lack of charity'. Moreover, further civil strife would weaken the power of England abroad. 'Our enemies want us divided, because we are now become a warlike nation, furnished with gallant men both by sea and land.'

Sincere repentance, he says, is the remedy. 'A real Reformation, private and public' (here again is the familiar note), 'with the punishment of crying sins, is very effectual to avert God's Judgement.' But Reformation seems very far off. Let us go back, he says, to our condition, 'before the Scots entered England with an army', and with 'searchings of humble hearts ponder what our duty is'. The *Politica Sacra et Civilis* is his attempt to answer this question.

The smaller, and, in composition, the later book against Hobbes strikes the same pious note, though with greater distinction. Government, Lawson insists, derives from Heaven. He was unwilling, he says, at first, to write against the *Leviathan*, 'tho' solicited'. For he thought Hobbes unimportant. Yet, since he was told by judicious friends, that the *Leviathan* 'took so much with many Gentlemen, and young Students in the Universities, and that it was judged to be a rational piece', he thought it 'profitable and convenient, if not necessary, to say something to the Gentleman [Hobbes], and did so'.

Here a passage already quoted from his introduction, will illustrate Lawson's quality. 'To think that the sole or principal Cause of the constitution of a civil State is the consent of men, or that it aims at no further end than peace and plenty, is too mean a conceit of so noble an effect. And in this particular I cannot excuse Mr. Hobbs ... and for this reason I undertake him.' Hobbes' definition of a commonwealth is equally applicable, he says, 'to a set of pirates'. Here is the same argument as that put forward by Rosse. It agrees with any 'unlawful multitude united to do mischief'. A Commonwealth, on the contrary, is 'a community of men orderly subjected to the supreme power civil, that they may live peaceably in all Godliness and honesty'.

This concern for decency and order, which contrasts with the irresponsibility and fanaticism of the more radical Puritans, was to be typically Whig. 'To glorify God and benefit man both by doing good and preventing and removing evil, should be the endeavour (as it is the duty), of every Christian in his station.' The flavour of smugness in the remark does not obscure its fundamental good sense. The affairs of this world, he says in his opening chapter, are all in the hands of God, who can lay the foundations of great empires and destroy them for their iniquity. But though God executes judgments when provoked, his general ordering of the world through the Laws of Nature tends to order and peace. War, it follows — and here he agrees with Filmer — far from being the natural condition of man, as Hobbes falsely argues, is unnatural. It is true that St. Paul 'brings in a bill of indictment against all mankind . . . *That their feet are swift to shed blood . . . and the ways of peace they have not known* (Rom. 3.15-17). Yet he understands this not of Nature but by corruption of Nature.'

For the sinners accused by St. Paul are civilized men, no longer in a state of nature, but under government. They are, indeed, corrupt, but their behaviour is irrelevant to Hobbes' argument that the state of nature is corrupt before government is in being.

As for Hobbes' 'Covenant of every one with every one for to design a Soveraign', it is 'but an Utopian fancy'. The development of society is gradual. From history we find 'that many States have attained to a settled form of Regular Government by degrees in a long tract of time, and that by several alterations'. Here is a remarkable idea in the seventeenth century, when the theory of contract was often interpreted so literally, and the sense of the past so rudimentary. Further, he says, civilized society, though ordained by God, is not deliberately planned. They come to it 'by a way fortuitous unto man'. Here, again, is a sophisticated view.

But Lawson has a more important aspect. He asserts the old doctrine of the trusteeship of power in a Commonwealth; and his analysis of sovereignty and its sanction is remarkable. Here is a direct link between medieval tradition and Locke, and something also of great significance, a doctrine of the separation of powers into Legislature, Judiciary and Executive. The sovereign power, he insists, resides in the community: the 'supreme Power Civil' is the 'first mover' in the State. This last phrase is medieval. From this power derive the Legislative, the Judicial and the Executive or administrative functions of government. This power is indivisible, otherwise there can be no 'first mover' in the State. Doctrines of sovereignty, coming down in part from Bodin in the 'seventies of the sixteenth century, have been assimilated by the middle of the seventeenth, though the full implications of Bodin are not accepted. Yet, 'for the administration', he says, 'it can be divided'. A king or ruler is not therefore the source of sovereignty, but a trustee. Here, already, is the fundamental Whig position.

Where, then, is the basis of the 'supreme Power civil' or 'first mover'? Lawson appears to find it in the original community. This is most directly to be found not in a Parliament, but, in England, in the 'fourty Counties'. He later reverts to this interesting theory. Men's first loyalty, he insists, 'is to be faithful to their Countrey'. (The word in seventeenth-century English can, of course, mean 'county' or 'locality'.) Then, and only secondly, comes his loyalty to the king, who swears to maintain the laws, liberty and religion by Law established. But this second loyalty 'cannot bind us to do anything against the Laws of God, of Nature, nor against our Countrey'. Here is something concrete as an alternative to the naked sovereignty of a ruler. Not merely an abstraction, such as the Law of nature, which Lucy, for example, rather feebly asserts, but the idea of the community, pinned down to 'our Countrey'. Add to this concept the sense of the continuity of tradition in Time, as well as its existence in space, and a point of view foreshadowing that of Burke is apparent. But in Hobbes' view, he says, 'every monarch is absolute'.

It follows that if a monarch violates his convenant of trusteeship, and 'perverts the main end of Government' one must resist him. But this must be done with caution, Lawson hastens to add, for sometimes even a tyrant is better than anarchy. Moreover, civil laws are not all-pervading. They can, and ought, to be by-passed in covenants with God like Baptism. Otherwise, he argues, rather quaintly, the covenant which the converted early Christians made with God, under the noses of heathen Emperors, could not have been valid.

This insistence on the spiritual side of covenants is reflected in his argument, before examined, against Hobbes' contention that 'covenants without the sword are but words and breath'. 'The principal force of a covenant,' says Lawson, in a fine phrase, 'depends on the will and consent of the immortal soul, which fears a deity and believes in a supreme judge of the world.' But as for 'the covenant of everyone with everyone, it is a mere chimera — there never was any such thing'. The power of sovereignty goes much further back than any such artificial covenant. In a commonwealth the community and the sovereign are the same. Tarquin in Rome was a tyrant, but the Romans asserted the power of the commonwealth when he was driven out. They then appointed 'executive officers, but not supreme'. All powers come from God and the community. The monarch or executive has a commission to protect the subjects, not to destroy them. An evil ruler who abuses his power may 'forfeit unto God by judgement, plague, war, etc.' He becomes *hostis humani generis*. Plainly if such rulers destroy their subjects, they must be expelled. 'If any man dare plead for these, let him, I dare not.' It was to be a topical phrase in the reprint of 1689.

Yet a prince cannot forfeit directly to his subjects. Rather he ceases to be a sovereign by a violation of duty, and his subjects cease to be subjects. It is when arguing against Hobbes' assertion that 'a prince may commit iniquity but not injustice', that Lawson makes the clearest assertion of his position by defining the 'Power Supreme Civil' already quoted. If a prince commits iniquity he is unjust. His commission from God gave him no power to commit injustice. Though a subject cannot, within the framework of the Laws, judicially accuse his prince, and though Lawson does not, of course, maintain that 'cursed rebels can murder princes', yet the framework of government can be dissolved. Power reverts to the original community. The prince, always supreme only for administrative purposes, can be expelled.

Lawson next defines the divisions of sovereign power. Hobbes, he says, falsely argues that the civil wars were provoked by the idea that power was divided between King, Lords and Commons. But where, says Lawson, is the supreme power? Not in the King. Of course, the 'cause moral' of these wars was our sins. And the 'political cause' was 'the male administration'. And obviously all sides have offended through want of wisdom and ignorance of politics in general. We do not, indeed, know for certain 'what the ancient constitution was', but we do know that the 'whole frame was strangely altered and corrupted'. And here he was voicing a very common opinion at the time. One finds it among the conservative but reforming lawyers, who looked back to a vague past of Anglo-Saxon freedom: and one finds it among the Levellers, for example in the writings of John Lilburne, with his idea that the ancient liberties of England had been subjected to the yoke of Norman 'colonels'.

Continuing his search for a basis for sovereignty, Lawson now reverts to his fruitful idea of the 'supreme Power radical' being in the forty counties. This concept links up with the projects for decentralization found, for example, in Milton's *Ready and easy way to Establish a Free Commonwealth*. This 'supreme Power radical', he maintains, ought to be exercised by King, Peers and Commons. Hobbes is quite wrong in attributing the Civil War to the assertion of this principle of division of power for executive efficiency. It should, moreover, be exercised according to 'certain rules which by Antiquaries in Law, together with some experienced States-men, might be found out, but are not'.[1]

This complaint that the whole constitutional question is not sufficiently studied, is very characteristic of Lawson. He is an exact scholar, who deplores the failure of clergy and laity to study politics. He goes on later, in another context, to complain that the historians of his day compare badly with those of Antiquity. Very few are skilled in Law, or statesmen of the calibre of 'Thucydides, Xenophon, Livy, Tacitus, Guicciardine, Commeignes and the like. These are men that could penetrate into the bowels of the state and discourse of the inward fabrick of the same'.

Further, he insists, political questions are obscured by misplaced religious passion. These fanatics are not truly religious, concerned with a Christian way of life. They are on a false scent and aim at civil power, not at 'spiritual liberty from sin'.

Here again, he argues, Hobbes, like other politically minded reformers is wrong in his approach. It is not by insisting on an absolute rule 'that all power civil must be

[1] p. 32.

one, as this author doth fondly fancy', that political and
social salvation will come about. It is, of course, the spirit
more than the form that counts. 'Let the form be the
best in the world, yet without God's governance it is
vain.' Nor is Hobbes' form even the best. Absolutism is
insidious and generally inefficient. And this can be shown
from history. 'And we know by experience,' Lawson
insists, 'that such as are only trusted with the exercise of
supreme power, will by little and little usurp it, and in
the end plead prescription. That is absolute and inherent
right.' So, he continues, Louis the Eleventh of France,
'when he violated the Laws of the constitution, removed
all such as by right ought to have poysed him.' The
word is characteristic, with its idea of balance. 'And
this,' he concludes, looking out over the European scene,
and the predominant absolutism of the mid-seventeenth
century, 'hath been the practice of the Princes of Europe
which in the end will prove their ruine.'

On a long term view his judgment was correct. Here
is a conscious and remarkable understanding of the value
of the growing tradition of compromise and constitutionalism, set against the predominant drift of continental
politics.

Such are the reflections made on Hobbes' attack on the
principle that King, Lords and Commons are together
aspects of a sovereignty deriving from the whole community.

Lawson then proceeds to criticize Hobbes' confusion
between a tyranny and a monarchy. Hobbes, he says,
maintains that tyranny and oligarchy are 'but different
names of Monarchy and Aristocracy, not different forms
of Governments'. This argument, Lawson rightly insists,

cuts across the whole tradition of medieval constitutionalism. Tyranny is a corruption of the state; a degeneration
caused by the 'wickedness of a prince and the faction of
an assembly ingrossing power'.[1] 'This man [Hobbes]', he
says, 'deserves to be a perpetual slave.' 'His intention is
to make men believe that the kings of *England* were
absolute Monarchs . . . the Parliaments of England
meerly nothing but shadows.' Lawson harks back to the
medieval distinction between a regal and a despotic power.
'Monarchy is regal over free men, despotical over slaves.'

In the late civil strife even zealots for the King condemned the absolutist doctrines of Sibthorpe, Manwering
and Martin.[2] 'For the English', he says boldly, in a
striking and memorable phrase, 'always desired to be
governed as men, not as Asses . . . This is the quality of
all understanding people of other nations.' Others, politically less reasonable, he wisely admits, are 'not capable of

[1] p. 36.
[2] Robert Sibthorpe, 1594-1662, royalist divine, Fellow of Trinity College, Cambridge,
1618, and Chaplain to the king. Preaching an assize sermon at Northampton in 1627 on
'Apostolick Obedience', he said: 'If princes command anything which subjects may not
perform because it is against the laws of God and nature, or impossible, yet subjects are
bound to undergo the punishment without either resistance or railing or reviling—and so
yield a passive obedience.' Archbishop Abbot refused to license the sermon and became
involved in controversy with Laud over it. Selden remarked of Sibthorpe's doctrine: 'If
that book be true, there is no *meum* and *tuum* in England.'
    Roger Manwering, Bishop of St. David's, was born in Shropshire in 1590. He was
educated at the King's School, Worcester, and became a Bible Clerk at All Souls. He
was appointed a chaplain to Charles I and preached that subjects could not refuse to pay
taxes 'without peril of damnation'. Pym said of him that 'he endeavoured to destroy the
king and kingdom by his Divinity'. He was imprisoned and fined by the Parliament in
1628, but Charles made him Dean of Worcester in 1633, where he was accused of popish
innovations. These included making the King's Scholars enter the Cathedral two by two
instead of jostling in pell mell, and being 'too social and jovial' for his office. In 1635 he
was consecrated Bishop of St. Davids, but was deprived and imprisoned by the Long
Parliament. He died in poverty at Carmarthen in 1653 and is buried at Brecknock.
    Edward Martin, Dean of Ely, was Provost of Queen's College, Cambridge. In 1642
he sent the college plate to the King. Ejected and sequestrated by Cromwell, he wrote a
'mock submission of the Covenant'. He escaped from London into East Anglia and
ultimately took refuge abroad. He was made Dean of Ely by Charles II and died in 1662.

a mild or moderated power'. Today, this distinction is familiar.

And here Lawson quotes Fortescue, 'the Chancellor'. The King of England, he said, 'hath not *regiam potestatem sed politicam, a populo effluxam*'. This quotation emphasizes the role of Fortescue in the development of Whig constitutionalism. No one with any sense, Lawson concludes, thinks the English monarchy was ever absolute. 'From all this everyone may see what little credit is to be given to *Arnisaeus* and *Besoldus*, and some other outlandish writers, who affirm the Kings of England to be absolute Monarchs.'[1]

Turning to Hobbes' assertion that monarchy is the best form of government, Lawson quotes the saying of a certain bishop against Bellarmine's argument for Papal supremacy. 'Purple', said the bishop, 'was the best colour, yet not best for the Cardinal's face.' Everything is right — in its proper situation.

Absolute power, Lawson again insists, is apt to provoke revolution. Yet he is careful, in the Whig manner, not to condone violence. 'To endeavour a change in a quiet state, and that out of ambition, or an humour of innovation, or an high conceit of their own state learning, will

---

[1] For Arnisaeus, see *Henningi Arnisaei Halberstadiensis, De Republica seu Reflectiones Politicae, Quorum Primus agit de civitate et familiis: Secundus de Rerum publ:* Frankfurt, 1615 (1187 pp.). This voluminous Teutonic writer treats of the errors of Keckermann (who confounds a *civitas* and a republic) and writes, misguidedly enough, of 'what democracy is'. See also his *De Auctoritate Principum in populum semper inviolabilis commentatio politica.*

Besoldus is most conveniently consulted in his short *Synopsis Politicae et Doctrinae.* Absolute power, he says, derives from God, *Quia non ab alio sed immediate a Deo dependit. Haecque ideo 'Sacrosancta' in jure nostro appeletur. Et nos etiam hodiei Imperium Romanum Sanctum 'Das Heilige Römische Reich', ut a Deo ordinatum* (BESOLDI, J. C., *Synopsis Politicae et Doctrinae,* 1628, de Majestate in Genere, p. 16). Besoldus wrote many works on political theory (*De Regimine sive statu monarchico,* 1618, etc.), but any claim to interest today must rest on his *Dissertatio de Bombardis ac item Typographia,* 1620. He also wrote a history of Jerusalem.

HOBBES AND HIS CRITICS

much offend God.' Alterations there must be made, but they should be made by consent of all parties, 'insensibly and little by little'.

He continues on the theme of the evil consequences of absolute power in a Commonwealth. Sovereign power, says Hobbes, ought in all Commonwealths to be absolute. Lawson agrees that it must be effective — obviously with the reservation that all power derives ultimately from the community — but insists that it is still strictly bound by the Laws of Reason, Nature and God, 'the only supreme and absolute lord of life'. If sovereigns dethrone themselves by abuse of their power, they bring a judgment on themselves for betraying God's trust. They may, indeed, alter the Laws, yet only 'so as all this tende to the publick good'. Here is the same view as that expressed, as will be seen later, by Hunton. 'For the end of Magistracie to set this out is no hard matter, if we consider what was looked at when God ordeyned it. That was the Good of the society of men over which it was set.'[1]

And of course Locke takes the same line, almost *verbatim.* 'Political power, then, I take it, to be the right of making Laws . . . and employing the force of the community to the execution of such Laws, and all this only for the public good.'[2]

The parallel with Lawson could not well be closer.

Following up this argument, Lawson again insists on the dangers of Hobbes' doctrine of unbridled power, and asserts one of the essential principles of political liberty. 'It is certain that princes desire to be Gods, absolute, independent, above all Laws . . . and to have the right to do wrong . . . And it is a dangerous thing to flatter them and

[1] See below, p. 103.   [2] *Treatise of Civil Government,* I, 3.

98

make 'em believe that their power is greater than it is, for it is the high way to Ruine.' Here, again, is the idea that absolutism does not pay. Liberty is essential to a healthy commonwealth.

And what do we mean by liberty? Not to be interfered with, says Lawson. In matters undefined by Law, a man is free. The subject is *liber*; and not only *liber* but *dominus*. He has not only *libertatem* but *potestatem*. Here is the same train of thought, fundamental to the Whig tradition, that a man is not guilty until he has been legally proved to be so, by proper process of Law. An idea still basic to Constitutional Government, foreign in many countries.

Ultimately, of course, says Lawson, true liberty is to be free from sin, from the dominion of our own desires. 'That is liberty divine.' Similarly, civil liberty is to be 'free from the lusts and imperious commands of absolute sovereigns, whose will, tho' irrational, and contrary to justice, must stand for Laws.' That is civil liberty. A man is 'Politically free when he is so far master of his life, goods, and children, and that which is justly his, that they can only be taken away from him, but for some crime contrary to just Laws'. Finally, he says, the liberty of a subject demands that 'he should not be compelled to do anything which a just man would not do if there were no Laws'.

The essentials of Lawson's doctrine have now been described. There is much more of it, and it is all ably argued. Here is a political thinker of very considerable calibre, to whom Locke was deeply indebted. Lawson was provoked by Hobbes' *Leviathan* to define political ideas which greatly strengthened the link between the tradition of Hooker and Fortescue (the adapted and Anglicized inheritance of Thomist and classical thought) — and the businesslike, modern teaching of Locke. For here are the essentials of this constitutionalism. The grasp of the necessity for sovereign power, but the insistence, also, that it reflects a wider order to which it is subordinate. The insistence that power comes from the community, and is even particularized in the forty counties. Finally, here is the most important idea of the division of the supreme power civil into Legislative, judicial and executive. Lawson is clearly a most formidable critic of Hobbes and something more than that. For in making his criticism he thinks constructively and with real statesmanship. These ideas, as already pointed out, are further developed in his other book, the *Politica Sacra et Civilis*. As Mr. Maclean rightly insists, mainly with reference to the larger work, there is a striking similarity of conception and emphasis. On the durability of civil society, on the capacity of political commonwealths, rightly conducted, to endure — on the precariousness of despotism. There is the same emphasis on trusteeship. Arbitrary power brings dissolution of government, but although Government is dissolved, civil society is not. There is a remedial power, deriving from God and natural Law and so inherent in the community. 'Mr. George Lawson', said the famous Puritan divine, Richard Baxter, 'the ablest man of almost any I know in England'; a man of 'methodical head, a man of great skill in politicks, wherein he is most exact'. Lawson must take his place in any future account of the development of the Whig tradition, and in the history of the long and successful assertion of the liberties of England.

There is much in common between the admirable pages of Lawson and the pamphlets of Philip Hunton. His contribution to the attack on Hobbes was indirect; but it is well worth glancing at a figure who played so important a part in the development of Whig political theory which was to form the core of resistance to the new doctrine. Hunton's two books had already provoked Filmer to write his best work, *The Anarchy of a Limited or Mixed Monarchy*, for they had caused him to 'scruple this modern piece of politicks'. And already, fourteen years earlier, Hunton had closely anticipated many of Lawson's arguments.

Some account of his life has already been given. His first book is entitled *A Treatise of Monarchie, . . . Done by an earnest Desirer of his Countrie's Peace*. It appeared in 1643.[1] The sequel, *A Vindication of the Treatise of Monarchy*, was published in the following year.

Hunton is an able writer. Though of lesser range than Lawson, he is much more formidable than Lucy. If he is less readable than Rosse, his political arguments are more exact. His style is dry and concentrated, with an almost scholastic touch. Here is a solid contribution to the tradition Hobbes was to attack, and against which his originality stands out.

The Treatise of Monarchie was written during the full crises of the Civil War and immediately provoked by it.

---

[1] Printed by John Bellamy and Ralph Smith . . . in Corn-hill, 79 pp.

Hunton also wrote a work called *Jus Regum*, now, apparently, lost. The first book is the more accessible, being reprinted, anonymously, in the sixth volume of the Harleian Miscellany. There is some account of him in MR. J. W. ALLEN's *English Political Thought 1603-1660*, and a very good article in PROFESSOR McILWAIN's *Constitutionalism and the Changing World*.

'What honest heart', he writes, 'doth not bleed to see the ruin of this late flourishing Kingdom go on so fast. Who can doe other than speak his mind? Suffer me to discover my heart in a case in which every honest man hathe a deepe interest.' Here is a real *cri de cœur*; a public-spirited attempt to check the violence that Lucy, with his plundered library, had deplored. And Hunton's book shows remarkable foresight. His remedy was constructive; one to which both sides had, in time, to come. For he understood that sovereign power works best through a mixed constitution. Here he is in line with Lawson's argument put forward fourteen years later, with the main Whig tradition. And here, like the rest of them, he is in direct opposition to Hobbes' argument for positivist sovereignty, derivative not from the community, but from a utilitarian compact which alone creates Law.

Hunton's argument is short and to the point: his style dry, precise and closely reasoned. His first book was designed in two parts. The first, 'Of Monarchy in Generall', is concerned with the nature of political government and of different kinds of monarchy, absolute and limited, elective and successive, simple and mixed. The second, 'Of this particular Monarchy', deals with the burning issue of the Civil War — 'Whether the power wherewith our Kings be invested be an absolute or limited and moderated Power.'

This important question is stated squarely in the first chapter of the second book — in 'The English Monarchy proved radically limited', and 'Contrary Arguments answered'. He then inquires whether the Constitution is 'Simple or Mixed', and proves it 'fundamentall mixed', and he asks whether the 'Estates' may resist the King.

The second book concludes with 'A moderate debate concerning the present contention' and with 'The speediest means of Reconcilement proposed'. Hunton's purpose was immediate and practical.

From these closely argued and rigorous pages two dominant ideas emerge. Both are antagonistic to the outlook of Hobbes. First that the central power, in the last resort, is limited by moral law and responsible for the welfare of the governed; secondly, that with a mixed constitution, it must provide the machinery for self-government. 'Government', he insists, 'is a moral power . . . it is to rule over men for the good of men.' 'For the end of Magistracie; to set this out is no hard matter, if we consider what was looked at when God ordeyned it. That was the Good of the society of men over which it is set.'[1] As Mr. Gough has pointed out, 'The trust concept is as fundamental in Hunton's political thought as it is in Locke's.'[2] Power, he insists, like Lawson and Locke, is trusteeship. 'It is the measure of all the acts of the Governor, and he is good or bad according as he uses his power to the good of the state wherewith he is entrusted.'[3]

Compare again Locke, who argues that an absolute prince has no place in civil society, but remains in an irresponsible state of nature, 'increased with power and made licentious with impunity'. These principles are clean contrary to the theories of arbitrary power then prevalent over most of the world and to be reinforced by Hobbes.

Moreover, Hunton had a clear grasp of the urgent pro-

---

[1] Chap. I, sect. II.   [2] J. W. GOUGH, op. cit., p. 152.
[3] Part I, i-ii.

103

blem of sovereignty. It is often said that Hobbes is the first English political theorist with a complete grasp of that doctrine. Yet here is Hunton, writing eight years before Hobbes' *Leviathan* appeared, saying 'Power of Majistracy . . . is one simple thing, an indivisible beam of Divine perfection.'[1] 'There is no accurate specific division of power, for it admits of none such, but partition of it according to diverse respects.' Here, in a nutshell, is an answer to one of the major controversies of the seventeenth century.

If we return to Hunton's moral argument, we find it thoroughly set out in the first book. Absolute monarchy exists 'when a people are absolutely resigned up, or resign up themselves to be governed by the will of one man'.[2] A limited monarchy is something radically different: 'not a stinted absolutism', but a power limited by external law. This legal power can only be conveyed by contract; and the ruler can have no more power than that which is given him by the contract. The people, when they made it, first had 'power over themselves and therefore had the right to set up their own terms'. Contract is, indeed, not normally revocable, otherwise monarchs were 'mere tenants at will'. But all power depends ultimately on consent. If the sovereign power inflicts 'mortal' injury on a society, and dissolves 'the frame of government and public liberty'; if 'petition fails', then the superior law of reason and conscience must be invoked. It is a 'power, not authoritative and civil, but moral, residing in reasonable creatures'. The people have transcended 'the frame of government they are bound to; they are unbound.'

[1] Chap. II, sect. III.　　　　[2] Chap. II, sect. I.

Hunton's second theme emphasizes the need for the executive to reflect the will of the whole commonwealth and provide the means of responsible self-government. He argues that the best arrangement is neither monarchy, aristocracy, or democracy, but a mixture of all three; of King, Lords and Commons, which will prevent 'crossing and jarring'. This is the only way out. 'Power should be exercised by those whom the Houses shall approve of.' It was just this question that in part provoked the Civil War; how to ensure that the executive reflected the will of the legislature, at that phase of social and economic development inevitably including both Houses of Parliament. Hunton, unlike Hobbes, believed that 'conciliation of interests' could best be brought about not by coercion but by consent.

His warning was timely; there was still a chance of compromise. At that stage the 'frame of government' was not yet dissolved. There was, indeed, no coercive power over the king; but Hunton begs him to come to a sensible compromise by 'condescent of grace'.

It was sound advice. He was, in fact, indicating the king's last chance. His suggestion was constructive; 'that His Majesty, for the sake of peace and present necessity of composing this distemperature, would be pleased to put himself upon the judgement and affection of the two Estates so assembled in their full bodies, and suspend the use of his negative voice, resolving to give his royall assent to what shall pass by the major part of the Houses freely voting'.

It was the obvious, the statesmanlike, solution. 'I am confident,' he concludes with sound common sense, 'if ever this War be transacted without the ruine of one side, which will endanger, if not undoe the whole, it must be by some such way of remission of rigour on both sides as I have now described.'

These are the main arguments of the *Treatise of Monarchie*. The outlook expressed is fundamentally opposed to the traditional patriarchalism of Filmer and also to the new stark authoritarianism of Hobbes. Though Hunton's argument is predominantly an anticipation of Locke, he invokes the old Tudor concept of 'condescent of Grace', repeated, it will be found, in Clarendon's criticism of Hobbes. His conception of society is organic, in striking contrast to the mechanical relations between governors and governed to be depicted in the *Leviathan*. It was a view significantly shared by moderates on both sides; on this ground Clarendon and Hunton meet — a notable example of English political good sense.

His less known *Vindication of the Treatise of Monarchy* is also worth examination. It recapitulates and develops some of his most closely reasoned and fundamental arguments, all incompatible with Hobbes' opinions.

The form of the pamphlet is very scholastic, with its strict tabulation; questions, determinations, assertions and objections. He goes to the root of what he calls the 'Vanity and Falsehood of the Supposals' (or premises) of contemporary controversy. These 'supposals' are wrong on four points; on sovereignty; on its limitation; on the means of limitation, and on the historical or actual constitution of the English monarchy. The argument is divided into five chapters and runs to thirty-one pages. It was written in answer to a pamphlet published by Dr. Henry Ferne, one of the King's chaplains, entitled *A reply unto Several Treatises pleading for the Armes now taken up by Subjects in the Pretended Defense of Religion and Liberty,* 1643.[1]

Hunton attacks the whole idea of hereditary right. 'Now I hold', he says, 'the negative to this question. Governing power is ordinarily conveyed to persons by public consent. This Public Consent is not only a mean but hath a causal influence.' To be sure, once that power is conveyed, the ruler must have authority to ensure the objective of all government — 'A peaceable life in all godliness and honesty.' But in its 'rule of acting', in execution, it must be limited. When the people consent to submit to government by rule of Law, they consent to something quite different from 'an unlimited power in the supreme'. In such societies power is limited 'in the very being and root of it'. Here is a bulwark against the Hobbesian doctrine that power creates Law.

Hunton quotes the authority of the Protestant Churches of Europe for the right to limit authority. Here is a notable example of the connection between the reformed religion and the assertion of political liberty, so much stressed by Figgis and many writers after him.

'I have,' he says, 'the judgement of all the reformed Churches and Divines in Germany, France, Belgium, Scotland, on my part, who have both allowed and actually used, forcible resistance against their sovereign's will.' Moreover, he continues, our own rulers have supported them. 'Yea, our own famous princes, Elizabeth, James, Charles I, both by Edict and assistance, have justified the

---

[1] Henry Ferne, D.D., 1602-62. Son of Sir John Ferne, the antiquary, one of the pioneers of Heraldic studies. He became Fellow of Trinity, Cambridge, in 1620 and in 1641 Archdeacon of Leicester. He was with the King at Carisbrook, and was appointed Master of Trinity at the Restoration. In 1661 he was made Dean of Ely and in 1662 Bishop of Chester, in which year he died.

same.' A limited power, he concludes, is not incompatible with efficiency. 'Limitation for a rule and defined way of working, I cannot see how it withstands the end of Government.' The Church carries on without a 'legislative power resident' to order or 'give authentick sense in matters *de fide*'. Yet she 'stands well enough' — an argument unpopular in high Anglican circles, let alone Catholic. So, he well says, a state might carry on by a 'compleat standing rule of Law' and a ministerial 'power of interpretation'. He repeats the argument in the *Treatise* that the sovereign power is in the King, Lords and Commons. Returning to the source of sovereignty, he maintains that in the original state of nature (and here his thought is as unhistorical as Hobbes') people 'resign themselves up by consent' and choose their Government. All depends subsequently on what kind of government they choose. If they choose absolutism, the power of the ruler in the subsequent society is unchecked: if a limited form of government, then nothing can take away its original limitation. For the people have an original or 'architectional' power to choose, before they are engaged in government.

As in Lawson's argument and Locke's, here is the insistence that sovereignty comes ultimately from the whole commonwealth, though this bridled sovereignty only occurs in states where the popular choice is for limited governments. Hunton thus concedes a good deal; later he abandons the wider doctrines of an effective universal natural law, narrowing his claim down to constitutional societies. For it is England he is primarily concerned about.

And he seems satisfied with this position. Here, he

concludes, is the fundamental idea 'of what I aver concerning God's ordinance in sovereignty, which I challenge to deny'. Proceeding in his argument, he next discusses the limitation of 'Majistracie'. There are, of course, the moral limits of Natural Law. But they are not very effective and apply to all societies. Then there are the civil or legal limits which operate in constitutional governments. If moral 'laws' are broken, the magistrate is overstepping the bounds of right or of 'sinless doing'. But he is not breaking the Law. For example, 'God's prohibition of eating swine's flesh did not take away from the Jews the natural power of eating it. They only lost the power of "sinless eating it".'

Thus, absolute government can and does break the moral Law, though there is no 'legal' check on it. But in a government limited by civil and legal restrictions the matter is different. Such restriction is not found in absolute monarchies. It 'induceth a real limitation of power, for sith it brings on illegality and unauthoritative Acts, exceeding' (if it exceeds). Legal limitation means a real diminution of power. Here it is *ratio formalis*, he says, using scholastic terms. Having defined the distinction between an absolute and limited Government, the next step is to prove that the English Monarchy belongs to the mixed or limited category. So the second chapter is concerned with the origin of the Monarchy, 'its limitation and mixture vindicated'. Hunton then goes back to the Saxon conquest. It was not, he insists, a conquest but rather an expulsion. For 'all the Britains which retained the name and nation' were expelled into Wales, 'as saith Mr. Cambden'. The Saxons 'came not into the condition of the conquered Britains, but they came into the old liberty of the Saxons'. This ingenious argument leads to an invocation of Tacitus, a tradition which went on and culminated, well worn, in the pages of Bishop Stubbs.

The argument of Tacitus, he says, is quite clear, 'and a record of more unquestionable authority than Tacitus I could not imagine — nor a more express testimony for the limited form in the very *potestas* of it of which sort, he affirms, the government of all the German nation was'. Moreover the Saxons, he hastens to add, were Germans. 'That they were a people of Germany before they came in hither is greatly probable.' Certainly, the 'Angli' who came with them were 'questionless Germans'. And since, he argues, applying Tacitus' description to all Germans in the best tradition of this school of argument, if the 'Angli' had limited monarchy, the Saxons would have had it. 'I endeavour', he admits, 'not to deduce the very model of our present Government . . . from the Saxon ingress.' But they were certainly organized in war bands in which the Kings had to consult their warriors, and they 'gave no tenure by conquest to their princes, but kept their Laws'.

Turning then to the 'Norman entrance' (he does not admit the word 'conquest'), Hunton denies that it subverted old liberties and insists on the slow development of Common Law, Hobbes' particular bugbear. On the development, too, of Parliament in a mixed constitution of King, Lords and Commons and on how far back that development goes. He compares the limitation of power in England with the arrangements in a college, using a similar comparison to that made by Fortescue. 'Thus in colleges the Fellows have an effectual though limiting power . . . though the Governour hath the power of calling and dissolving their meetings, yet they have a power of limiting, nay, censuring him from exhorbitance.' Hunton's academic experience may have given him ground for this example.

Finally, he argues, reverting to the main theme of the difference between a legal limitation and a mere moral *caveat*, is it likely that so much effort would have been spent in securing Magna Carta if it was not a practical document? 'I ask, when the liberties of Magna Carta were recovered with so much trouble, expense and blood, whether, by all this ado, was intended only a moral liberty?'

The last three chapters of the *Vindication* are concerned with the immediate crisis, with the Right of Resistance. All government, he insists, depends ultimately on consent, on public opinion. Even in absolute monarchies the King has to rely on the force of his subject's arms. And if he destroys the State, his subjects will resist him. How much the more a resistance is justified in a limited Monarchy! 'From the lawfulness of resistance of unreasonable acts of will in an absolute monarchy, where reason is the Prince's Law, I may *a fortiori*, conclude the lawfulness of Resistancy of instruments of illegal acts in a limited Monarchy where the Law of the Land is the Prince's Law and Bounds.'

Hunton does not advocate resistance by private individuals, but by constitutional means. This is legitimate: 'raised by defenders of law, a rebellion raised by magistrates, having authority, against instruments of Arbitrariness, having no authority'. He concludes, with a touch of Puritan fervour: 'If ever Reasons did demonstrate a Truth, I am confident these four have made good the power of the Estates in Parliament to resist subversive instruments, be they more or few, as Phil. 4.5. "Let your moderation be known unto all men. *The Lord is at hand.*" '

Hunton's argument on the actual limitation of power by legal means is the particular contribution of both his books. The concept of Natural Law is invoked, but he is a practical man. He realizes that law is not law unless it can be enforced; that power must be limited by institutions. And this insistence of the importance of institutions makes him analyse carefully how the English method of government should actually work, and insist on the importance of a mixed government. Hunton therefore reinforces the basic traditional concept of the general trusteeship of power with precise suggestions for its realization. That these suggestions should have been made as early as 1643 is remarkable, and shows how clearly the tradition of Lawson and Locke goes back. Both indirectly, as asserting principles clean contrary to those set out by Hobbes, as well as by the royalist defenders of the monarchy, and directly, as contributing to the main stream of English political thought, Hunton deserves attention. In the words of an American writer, 'Hunton's distinctive merit is not merely his lucid analysis of past and present theory; it is in his prophetic recognition of the corporate character of sovereignty in England.'[1]

Such were the ideas already current thirteen years before Lawson's attack on Hobbes. Hunton's argument had greatly reinforced the idea of government by consent; it was Hobbes' attack on that principle which was to win him so much unpopularity with the more 'advanced' thinkers of the left. It will be apparent from Hunton's

[1] D. BUSH, op. cit., p. 236.

vigorous and exact argument how powerful a tradition was already in being before Lawson so ably summed it up, developed it and brought it to bear on a new and outrageous adversary. For where Hunton's opponents had been royalists — Ferne, and later Filmer — Lawson was confronted with something strange. The supporters of the King asserted a traditional patriarchalism; in controversy with them it was possible for Hunton to retain something in common with his enemies. But Lawson was to wield the weapons forged by the controversies of the civil wars against the fundamental denials of a writer ultimately hostile both to the Whig and the royalist position; one who denied the basic premises and sanctions on which that position was built.

CHAPTER VI

BISHOP JOHN BRAMHALL'S
CATCHING OF THE LEVIATHAN

TURNING from the sober Whiggish argument of George Lawson and Philip Hunton, to the baroque eloquence of John Bramhall, Bishop of Derry, afterwards Archbishop of Armagh, one reverts to the world of Jacobean polemical learning. The close semi-scholastic method of exposition, with its carefully tabulated headings, the sober constructive purpose, the desire to 'do good' in the 'fear of the Lord', gives place to a more worldly method of debate. This old-fashioned atmosphere, reminiscent of the wide erudition of Rosse, is shot through with the forensic skill of a prelate versed in the ways of court and bureaucracy. Here is an example of the high spirited 'cavalier' attack on Hobbes, from the 'Right', just as the home-spun prose of Lawson represents the Whig-Puritan attack from the moderate 'Left'.

The author is a well-known figure in the church history of his time. A florid, formidable character, his career was precisely what one would imagine from the tone of his book. He early made a prudent marriage to a clergyman's widow, which 'gave him a fortune and a library'. As we have seen, in 1623 he was appointed Chaplain to Tobias Mathew, Archbishop of York. In 1633 he went to Ireland as Chaplain to Wentworth, and lost no time in getting promotion there, being made in that year Archdeacon of Meath, the richest Archdeaconry in Ireland, and in the following year, Bishop of Derry.

As Archdeacon of Meath he at once set himself to put the chaotic finances of the Irish Church in better order. By obtaining the surrender of fee farms let out at a loss, he saved the Irish Establishment £30,000 a year; later, as Bishop of Derry, he augmented the income of his diocese.[1] He was equally hostile to the Roman Catholic Southern Irish and to the Ulster Presbyterians. He opposed, without success, the project for allowing the Southern Irish a prayer book in their own language, and attempted, with results which can be imagined, to make the Ulster Scots abjure the covenant. In his attack on the Presbyterians he worked in concert with a Somerset man, John Atherton, Bishop of Waterford and Lismore, who was educated at Gloucester Hall and Lincoln College, Oxford, who also went over to Ireland with Wentworth; and who came, in 1640, to an end so scandalous as to be outstanding in the annals of the Church of Ireland, being hanged, to the edification of a Dublin mob, in circumstances of peculiar ignominy.[2]

During the crisis which led up to the civil wars, Bramhall tried to maintain his position in Ireland, where he had invested in large properties in County Tyrone, but he retired to England in 1641 and did his best for the cause of the King. He was present at the battle of Marston Moor, after which he fled to Hamburg. He was known to the Puritans as 'Bishop Bramble' and Cromwell called

[1] In the *Calendar of State Papers (Ireland)*, 1634, p. 88, it is recorded 'In my own Diocese of Derry, I found the annual rents at £760 and £100 for mensals and fishings. By a compromise with the tenants, I raised it to about £1400 in rents and a fair desmesne at Londonderry, and the fishing doubled at least.' These transactions would seem to be the beginning of a gradual augmentation which went on until the Bishopric of Derry was the wealthiest of all episcopal and archiepiscopal Sees, except that of Armagh. As late as 1833 the stipends were: Armagh, £17,669; Derry, £14,193; Dublin, £9320.

[2] See WOOD, vol. II, BLISS, p. 892, and BERNARD, NICHOLAS, *A Relation of the Penitent Death of Bishop Atherton* (1641).

him the 'Irish Canterbury'. His affinities with Laud were indeed obvious. He remained in exile in Germany, France and the Low Countries, meeting Hobbes (his senior by six years) in Paris, where, as we have seen, he debated the problems of 'Liberty and Necessity' which gave rise to the publication in 1658 of his *Castigation of Mr. Hobbes*, to which the *Catching of the Leviathan* forms a sequel.

After various vicissitudes, which included a hurried visit to Cork, and apparently an expedition to Spain, he returned at the Restoration; in 1660 he was consecrated Archbishop of Armagh. He died of a stroke in Court when arguing a matter of litigation about his Irish properties.

Bramhall left upon his contemporaries an impression of ability and drive. He was an administrator and man of affairs, a many-sided, able and often hasty controversialist.[1] His book against Hobbes, as has been indicated, was the result of a prolonged dispute arising out of metaphysical arguments canvassed in the circles frequented by Hobbes and Bramhall in Paris.

Bishop Vesey's opinion of it has already been quoted; 'Good judges', he said, 'have thought he [Hobbes] hath not licked himself well of those wounds the Bishop of Derry gave him . . . We are told,' he adds, 'by the noble Du Plessis that it is the concept of the later Jews that the Leviathan is a dainty dish, seasoned and reserved by God

---

[1] There is an interesting letter from his hand written to Archbishop Ussher in 1654, in which he warns the Archbishop of a Catholic plot to fish in the troubled waters of radical discontent in England. It shows that his hatred of Popery was as intense as his dislike of the Presbyterians. The Catholics, he warned the Archbishop, were plotting, in 1646, to attain Toleration (as in Holland), by fomenting agitation in the Army, and for this end were actually prepared to connive at the murder of the King. *Harleian Misc.*, vol. VII, pp. 509-10 (Ed. 1746).

for the entertainment of the Messias and his friends; but, sure, this can be none of it, for the foul beast hath such an "haut goust" that Christians have no stomach for it here, and I suppose their appetites will be no more carnall at the Resurrection.'

Vesey's assessment of Bramhall's attack is borne out by a study of the text. In a style which combines a complex Jacobean eloquence with the racy wit of the Restoration, Bramhall brings the shrewd judgment of a man of the world to bear on Hobbes' theoretical dogmatism.

The Catching of the Leviathan first appeared in 1658. The full title of the first edition runs: *The Catching of the Leviathan, or the Great Whale. Demonstrating out of Mr. Hobbs his own Works, That no man who is thoroughly an Hobbist, can be a good Christian, or a Good Common-wealths man, or reconcile himself to himself. Because his Principles are not only destructive to all Religion but to all Societies; extinguishing the Relation between Prince and Subject, Parent and Child, Master and Servant, Husband and Wife; and abound with palpable contradictions,* by John Bramhall, D.D. and Bishop of Derry. Proverbs: xii, 19. *'The lip of truth shall be established for ever but a lying tongue is but for a moment.'* [1]

The book is bound up with Bramhall's larger *Castigation of Mr. Hobbes his last Animadversions in The Case concerning Liberty and Universal Necessity,* to which it forms an appendix. It was reprinted in the Collected Edition of Bramhall's Works, which appeared in Dublin in 1676, with a life of Bramhall by Vesey, and in the 1677 edition, *The Catching of the Leviathan* forms a third discourse of the third tome of the collected works; it is divided into

---

[1] London, 1658. Printed for E.T. by John Crooke. At the Sign of Ship, St. Paul's Churchyard.

three chapters which cover pages 869-903. It attacks Hobbes' theology and political theory as set out in the *De Cive* and the *Leviathan*.

The first chapter criticizes Hobbes' religious views but trenches on politics; the second is an onslaught on his political principles; the third attempts to prove his arguments inconsistent with one another. Hobbes' *Answer* tries to refute the first chapter, with its charge of atheism, in detail, but only the first.[1] The second chapter, which contains a more devastating attack, Hobbes arrogantly considered not worth a reply. He writes 'As for the second chapter, which includes my civil doctrines, since my errors there, if there be any, will not tend very much to my disgrace, I will not take the pains to answer it.'[2] Nor did he answer the third chapter, with its charges of inconsistency. He turned to his 'Narrative concerning Heresy', to prove that the government had no right to burn him as a heretic.

Bramhall's main contention was that Hobbes' religious views were intolerable and subversive; the political attack was subsidiary. In his preface 'to the Christian Reader', he argues that Hobbes is an Atheist for equating God with Nature, and that the Leviathan is a Phantasm. Hobbes, he says, is overbearing, but 'our great Leviathan hath his sufferings'. He cites the vulnerability of the elephant to the mouse, which runs up its trunk and eats its brain so that the animal dies mad, and the story of the Indian rat and the crocodile.[3]

'Our Greenland fishers', Bramhall continues, 'have found out a new art to draw him out of his castle . . . with

---

[1] See HOBBES, *Collected Works*, Ed. Molesworth, vol. IV, pp. 281-384. (*An Answer to a book published by Doctor Bramhall, late Bishop of Derry*, etc.)

[2] HOBBES, op. cit., p. 384.　　　　　　[3] Compare Rosse, above, p. 62.

their harping irons, and by giving him line and space enough to bounce and tumble up and down and tire himself out and try all his arts, as spouting up a sea of water to drown them, and striking at their shallops with his tail to overwhelm them; at last to draw this formidable creature to the shore or to the ship, and slice him in pieces and boil him in a cauldron and tun him up in oil.' This striking simile is very characteristic of Bramhall's mind; he takes a topical aspect of the obvious lead given by Hobbes' title, and works it out with elaborate precision.

'I have provided', he continues, 'three good harping irons for myself to dart at this monster. The first is aimed at his heart or theological aspect; the second at his chine, or political part; the third is aimed at his head, or rational part of his discourse . . . Let him take heed, if these three darts do pierce Leviathan his house, not all the Dittany which groweth in Creet[1] that can make them drop easily out his body, without the utter overthrow of his cause.' *Haerebit lateri lethalis arundo*. The lethal arrow will stick in his side.

The first chapter, That the Hobbesian Principles are destructive of all Christianity and Religion, is more generally known than chapters two and three. As before indicated, it is extensively quoted by Hobbes. It concludes: 'if his disciples have such an implicit faith that they can digest all these things, they may feed with ostriches'.

The following and less known chapter begins effectively, 'The first harping iron is thrown into the heart of the great whale . . . now let him look to his chine.' This

[1] Dittany was called 'Dictannus Creticus'. 'And from the wod of Mount Ida in Creit/ Up hes scho pullit dictain, the herb sweit.' GAWIN DOUGLAS, *Aenies*, 1513. (See *Oxford English Dictionary*.)

and that sovereign princes are in a 'posture of gladiators' is to make the worst of the situation. They are not, in fact, constantly at war, and when they do go to war they declare it with due formality beforehand.[1]

Here Bramhall is not upon firm ground, either in his own age or in our own. The arguments of the *Leviathan*, he says, are shocking in the context. According to Hobbes' principles there is no need to declare war on one's enemies; it is lawful to cut their throats without warning. But the Romans, says Bramhall, doubtfully, always observed the decencies of the laws of war.

He then turns to some of the internal implications of the *Leviathan*. Hobbes is unpractical, he insists again, in his recommendations for defence. Bramhall scouts the theory that 'men of feminine courage' should be exempt from military service except in extreme emergencies, when all have to bear arms. And this last contingency is impossible. 'He must be a mortal God indeed that can bring all the hands in a kingdom to fight in one battle.' Bramhall was mercifully unaware of modern progress in total war.

He proceeds to a statesmanlike and realist argument, on the implications of Hobbes' religious doctrines in the dangerous situation of the time. One of the worst problems which faced governments in the mid-seventeenth century was how to stabilize the aftermath of the wars of religion. The Thirty Years War was only ten years over, and as late as 1688 the bigotry of James II was matched by the intolerance of Calvinist Huguenot writers.[2] Only

---

[1] Compare Lucy's argument, above, p. 81.
[2] See J. H. DODGE, *The Political Theory of the Huguenots of the Dispersion* (New York, 1947), which deals particularly with the writings of Jurieu, the advocate of a 'Protestant Inquisition'.

reluctantly, as a political manœuvre, were such fanatics induced to admit of toleration. Bramhall had experienced the fanaticism of Irish Catholics and Ulster Protestants; he knew what a powder magazine Hobbes' insistence on religious conformity would set off. His political judgment was extremely sound. Although a Prelate of the Anglican Church, he is quite clear that from an administrative point of view wide toleration was necessary. And he is shrewd to set Hobbes' religious doctrines in their political context.

Hobbes' totalitarian outlook in religion, he insists, is extremely dangerous. 'We see the present condition in Europe, what it is; that most sovereigns have subjects of different communion from themselves, and are necessitated to tolerate different rites, for fear lest while they are plucking up the tares, they should eradicate the wheat. And he that should advise them to do otherwise doth advise them to put all to fire and flame. To hear this merciful and peaceable author; "It is manifest that they do against conscience . . . who do not cause such doctrine and worship to be taught their subjects as they themselves believe".' Both Hobbes' hypocrisy and lack of statesmanship are here obvious. 'Did this man writ waking or dreaming?'

As in the passage about Arithmetic and Geometry, Bramhall here brings the experience of a man versed in affairs to reveal the practical implications of Hobbes' argument. He proceeds to the obvious practical weaknesses of Hobbes' idea of unbridled sovereign power. And besides, in spite of his views on absolutism, Hobbes legalizes rebellion. 'No man is bound by his pacts . . . not to resist him who bringeth upon him death or wounds

123

or other bodily dammage,' he writes. But 'by this learning', says Bramhall, 'the Schollar, if he be able, may take
the rod out of the master's hand and whip him'. Why not,
he asks, change the name of *Leviathan* into 'Rebel's
catechism'?

As for the argument that the obligation of subjects
ceases when the sovereign cannot protect them, it is
absurd and subversive. Protection ought to be mutual.
'By his leave, this is right dogs play, which always takes
part with the stronger side. It seemeth Mr. T. H. did
take his sovereign for better but not for worse.' Here in
a telling and homely phrase is a shrewd hit at one of
Hobbes' particularly subversive theories. One convenient
enough at the time perhaps for Hobbes personally, but a
principal cause of the distrust in which he was held by
both parties.[1] And indeed, one of the most flagrant
weaknesses of the Hobbesian State would be its failure to
command confidence, and this failure has been again and
again the cause of the downfall of governments con-
structed on Hobbesian lines. It has always been a
principal strength of the constitutionalist position, resting
on respect for the individual and appealing to consent,
that it has commanded a loyalty which the doctrine of
calculating self-interest, which 'takes the sovereign for
better and not for worse' — (what a good phrase it is!) —
can never of its nature provide. It is the measure of a
State's vitality that such 'dogs play' is not prevalent.

Bramhall goes on to insist that there is no such thing
as the state of nature envisaged by Hobbes. 'There was
never any such degenerate rabble of men in the world

[1] As Professor Basil Willey remarks: '... not the vicar of Bray himself could more
decisively subordinate speculative truth to practical considerations than Hobbes....'
op. cit., p. 112.

that were without all religion, all government, all laws natural and civil; no, not among the most barbarous Americans, who (except for some criminal habits) have more principles of natural piety and honesty than are readily to be found in his writings.'

He proceeds to attack another fundamental Hobbesian doctrine, that the principles of civilized society reflect no divinely sanctioned natural Law, or, for that matter any moral principles valuable as a tried rule of conduct tending to betterment of life. Such principles, says Hobbes, are merely the reflection of convenience, purely utilitarian. Naturally this view that the state is merely a forcible 'conciliator of interests', offends a prelate of the Anglican Church. Indeed, Hobbes' negative utilitarianism is unlikely to command loyalty in a commonwealth. It can give only a negative security, and even that Hobbes' principles are unlikely to achieve. This blindness to moral values, the lack of constructive vision, he implies, is one of the gravest limitations of Hobbes' outlook.

In comparing the laws of the Commonwealth to the neutral laws of 'gaming', Bramhall continues, Hobbes subverts the Law of Nature and his 'Oekonomics' are no better than his politics. Further, parental power is destroyed and the subordination of wives to their husbands undermined. Finally, says Bramhall, 'his faults do come so thick I am weary of observing them . . . Take an Hotch-potch together'. And he does so, under nine headings. 'Thus,' he concludes the second chapter, 'after a view of his religion, we have likewise surveyed his politics; as full of black, ugly dismal rocks as the former, dictated with the same magesterial authority. Man may judge them to be twins on the first cast of an eye . . . Mr.

T. H. taketh a pride in removing all ancient landmarks, between Prince and subject, father and child ... Nilus after a great overflowing doth not leave such a confusion after it as he doth; nor an Hog in a Garden of Herbs.'

Following this vivid and memorable phrase, the third chapter is concerned with Hobbes' inconsistency. 'This harping iron is aimed at the head of his Leviathan, or the rational part of his discourse ...' Hereditary Government, says Hobbes, is the best. Yet he argues that the Sovereign can dispose of it. 'Law he calls the "Dictate of right reason": at another time he sayeth there are no laws.' That the Law of Nature is only an understanding of what should and should not be done, while law has coercive power. 'Speaking properly,' he argues, 'they are not laws as they proceed from nature.' He calls laws 'eternal and immutable', but maintains 'They do not oblige as laws before there be a commonwealth constituted. When a Commonwealth is actually settled then are they actually laws and not before.' Here, indeed, Hobbes attempts to have it both ways. Having written off the traditional Law of Nature and made all law simply the command of a superior, saying in fact that 'might is right', he invokes certain characteristics of human conduct as Laws of 'Nature', backing up his manmade state. Here Bramhall has struck accurately at an obvious target.[1] Again, 'He sayeth the Institution of Eternal punishment was before sin,' and, further, 'if the command be such as cannot be obeyed without being damned to eternal death, then it were madness to obey it.' 'Yet at other times he sayeth there is no eternal

[1] See below, Whitehall, p. 180.

punishment.' In a phrase worthy of Donne, Bramhall comments, 'He that knoweth nor soul nor spirit may well be ignorant of a spiritual death.'

After enumerating other inconsistencies, the chapter concludes by reverting to an attack on the two basic aspects of Hobbes' position; his ideas of the State of Nature and of Sovereignty. 'A principal cause of his errors is fancying to himself a general state of nature which is so far from being general, that there is no instance to be found of it in the nature of things, where mankind was altogether without laws and without governours, guided only by self interest, without any sense of conscience, justice, honesty or honor. He may search all the corners of America with a candle and Lanthorn at noon-day and after his fruitful pains, return a *Non est inventus*. Perhaps, indeed, an "odd handful of men" might, through degeneration, become "more brutish than the beasts themselves", but would any man in his right wits make that to be the universal condition of mankind? . . . or that to be the state of Nature which is . . . but an accidentall degeneration?'

Here is a similar argument to that invoked by Lawson, who, it will be remembered, insists that when St. Paul brings in a 'general bill of indictment against all mankind', he is dealing with man in civilized communities, not in the state of nature.[1]

'A second ground of his erroure,' Bramhall continues, reverting to his previous argument, 'is his gross mistake of the Laws of Nature . . . A moral Heathen would blush for shame to see such a catalogue of the Laws of Nature. First he maketh the Laws of Nature to be laws and no

[1] See above, p. 90.

laws; not laws but theorems, laws which required not
performance but endeavours, laws which were silent, and
could not be put into execution in the state of nature,
where all things were defined by a man's own judgement
and ... where there were no public judgements and no
use of witnesses' ... 'Every one of these grounds,' he
continues, 'here alleged are most false, without any
verisimilitude in them, and so his superstructure must
needs fall flat to the ground.' Here is a fair description
of Hobbes' views on natural law. The contrast between
mere 'endeavour' and execution, which can only be
achieved by sovereign state power, being particularly apt.

Finally the Bishop becomes eloquent in the old pulpit
style of the early seventeenth century. Hobbes, he says,
'maketh the onely end of all the laws of nature to be "the
long continuation of a man's life and members" — most
untruely. He maketh every man by nature the onely
judge of his own conversation; most untruely ... He
sayeth the natural condition of mankind is "a war of all
against all" most untruely; that nature dictateth to a man
"to retain the right of preserving his life and limbs against
a lawful magistrate", lawfully proceeding; most untruely.
I omit his uncouth doctrine about pacts made in a state
of nature ... These things are unsound, and the rest of
his laws, for the most part poor trivial things in comparison with those weightier dictates of nature which he
hath omitted.'

Hobbes' view, he continues, like the other critics, is
profoundly unorthodox. An arrogant assertion of a dogmatic and narrow-minded writer, scorning the wisdom of
the past. All other writers of politics, Bramhall insists,
'do derive Commonwealth from the sociability of nature,

which is in mankind, most truely. But he will have the beginning of all humane society from mutual feare. We see some kind of creatures delight altogether in solitude, rarely or never in company. We see others (among which is mankind) delight altogether in company, rarely or never in solitude. Let him tell me what mutual feare of danger did draw the silly bees into swarms; or the sheep or doves into flocks . . . and I shall conceive it possible that the beginning of humane society might be from feare also'. This argument has been used by the earlier critics, though less precisely.

Finally, Bramhall attacks the central bastion of Hobbes' doctrine, his theory of sovereignty. Significantly, he regards it as an innovation. 'Thus,' he proceeds, 'having invented a fit foundation for his intended building, Yclept "the state of meer nature" . . . he hath been long modelling a new form of polity to be builded upon it; but the best is, it hath onely been in paper. And all the while he hath never had a finger in mortar.' Hobbes' lack of political and administrative experience is again emphasized. 'This is the new frame of absolute Sovereignty,' Bramhall continues, 'which Mr. T. H. knew right well we could never let stand, nor he should ever be permitted to reer up in our European climates, or in any other part of the habitable world which had ever seen any form of civil government. Therefore, he hath sought out a fit place in America, among the savages, to try if perhaps they might be persuaded that the names of good and evil, just and unjust doe signify nothing but at the pleasure of the sovereign Prince.' Here, it will be observed, Bramhall, like all the other critics, takes for granted that there is a tradition of government, generally accepted and estab-

field of political action. And Bramhall's second successful contribution is a statesmanlike understanding of the appalling contemporary consequences of Hobbes' suggested subordination of religion to the State. 'We see the present condition of Europe, what it is . . . Did this man writ waking or dreaming?' This point is still worth pondering to everyone who, disregarding Hobbes' historical context, thinks his evasive doctrines were practical politics. They would, indeed, have 'put all to fire and flame'. The toleration Locke was to advocate proved a greater achievement of the decades after Hobbes' death: Bramhall had the vision to foresee its necessity.

His other point, that the name of *Leviathan* ought to be 'Rebel's Catechism', shows up a more obvious and familiar weakness of Hobbes' position — the instability, the psychological inadequacy, of government based on a mere calculation of advantage, devoid of sentiment and tradition, and not based on free consent. But where else is that weakness better emphasized? 'By his leave, this is right dogs play, which always takes part with the stronger side. It seemeth Mr. Hobbes doth take his sovereign for better but not for worse.' This point has been seldom better put.

Here are three effective criticisms which drive home the second harping iron into the Leviathan's chine.

As to the third, or rationalized attack — the attack on Hobbes' inconsistency — that is perhaps easier game. But it is effectively dealt with. Forging through a welter of minor inconsistencies, Bramhall concentrates on the weakness of Hobbes' view of Natural Law, on his alleged state of nature, and on his theory of sovereignty.

Hobbes makes the Laws of Nature, 'laws that are silent. A moral heathen would blush for shame to see such a catalogue of the Laws of nature'. Yet, having shown that these Laws are 'silent' in a state of nature, he brings them in again to support his artificial commonwealth. Such laws are no laws — it is a familiar argument.

The Hobbesian conception of sovereignty is even more artificial. 'This new frame of absolute sovereignty which Mr. T. H. knew right well we would not have let stand nor he should ever be permitted to reer up in our European climates.' Bramhall here asserts that such doctrines are inefficient — a most telling and permanent argument against arbitrary methods of government. 'Mr. T. H.', he says, 'hath never had a finger in mortar.' He does not know what his doctrine implies. Secondly, he insists, that they are incompatible with English, and even with predominant European, tradition. Few of the other critics so specifically extend the indictment to this European scale, though they invoke the vague idea of world citizenship.

It is not, therefore, only for his debating skill, his power of phrase — ('an Hog in a Garden of Herbs') — but his statesmanlike understanding of the implications of the *Leviathan* that Bramhall must be rated among the ablest of contemporary critics of Hobbes. Though a high Church Bishop, one feels he was no fanatic; rather, like the rest of them, a man of sense.

CHAPTER VII

THE TWO DIALOGUES OF
DR. JOHN EACHARD

T HE criticism of Hobbes now to be examined is couched in very different terms from any of the attacks hitherto described. The Reverend John Eachard brought to the controversy the outlook of a generation younger than Hobbes or Rosse, Lucy or Lawson. He had a robust and ordinary mind and a power of banter as well as of invective. It was not until 1672 that he wrote the first of his racy knockabout *Dialogues*. With its sequel in 1673, it is the most entertaining of the works under consideration, and one of the most effective of all the attacks on Hobbes.

John Eachard was a Suffolk man of substantial family. He was admitted Fellow of St. Catherine's College, Cambridge, in 1658: he became Master in 1675, two years after the publication of the Second Dialogue. He was a vigorous and popular head of his house and a good administrator, being twice Vice-Chancellor of the University of Cambridge, in 1679 and 1695. He died in 1697, having rebuilt the front of his College and leaving all his money to the society.[1]

Dr. Eachard is better known than the rest of these critics except Clarendon, for in 1670 he had written a

---

[1] The best edition of his works was printed in the eighteenth century: *A Complete Collection of the Works of John Eachard*, D.D., *Late Master of Katherine Hall and Vice Chancellor of the University of Cambridge* (London, 3 vols., printed for T. Davies in Russell Street, Covent Garden, 1783).

spirited and wise little book on the *Grounds and Occasions of the Contempt of the Clergy*. Macaulay made use of the work, and by it Eachard is known to scholars, but his books against Hobbes, though popular in the eighteenth century and compared by Dryden to the *Dialogues* of Fontenelle, have fallen into an undeserved neglect. This pamphlet about the clergy, is, indeed, worth a short consideration before turning to the main work, for it illustrates Eachard's personality.[1]

The preface strikes much the same note as the attack on Hobbes. Eachard remarks that he is no reformer; he is not posing as a 'Saint or worthy', but wants decency and order. Similarly, it will be found, his objective in discrediting Hobbes is social rather than intellectual. Many ordinary young men are being corrupted by Hobbes' doctrines; he writes to attract their attention, rather than to embark on learned and high-minded disputation.

The causes for the contempt in which many of the Clergy were held in the middle seventeenth century are twofold — ignorance and poverty. He divides his argument accordingly. Under ignorance comes a discussion, singularly enlightened, of the limitations of the University curriculum. He asks 'whether it be unavoidably necessary to keep lads to sixteen or seventeen years of age, in pure slavery to a few Greek and Latin Words?' Could not the authorities try mixing this 'starched' learning with something that would 'take better with

---

[1] *The Grounds and Occasions of the Contempt of the Clergy and Religion enquired into in a letter written to R.L.* (131 pp., printed for Mr. Godbid and M. Brooke at the Angel in Cornhill, 1670). It provoked *An answer to a letter of enquiry into the Grounds and occasions of the contempt of the Clergy*, to which Eachard replied in another pamphlet of about the same size. He was, therefore, busy writing from 1670 to 1673, when the *Dialogues* against Hobbes were also written.

them'? They might, for example, study some English authors, whereby they could 'Come in a short time to apprehend common sense and begin to judge what is true.' Further, they might even be *encouraged*, 'for most certainly youths, if handsomely dealt with, are much inclinable to emulation'. As things are, 'What pleasure do we think can such a one take in being bound to get against breakfast two or three hundred rumblers out of Homer in Commendation of Achilles' toes?' After these sensible remarks, which had no effect on the University authorities at the time, Eachard criticizes the method of recruiting the Clergy — 'the inconsiderate sending of all kinds of lads to the Universities', and the poor treatment many of these sizars receive in the Colleges. 'It is ten times more happy both for the lad and for the Church to be a corn cutter, or a tooth drawer, to make or mend shoes, or to be of any inferior profession,' than to 'be had up to the University' only to be made to 'buy eggs and butter.' As for most of them, 'having exactly learned *Quid est logica*, etc., down they go by the first carrier, upon the top of his Pack, into the West or North. What a champion for truth is such a thing likely to be?' These half educated parsons are not likely to bring much credit on the Cloth.

The other kind which bring their calling into contempt are the over-sophisticated Clergy. 'With what elaborate heights and tossing nonsense will they greet a right down English father or Country friend?' And when, in the rural pulpit, 'he thinks he hath catched one of his old school questions, and so falls to slinging it this way and that; he lets it run a little, then, *Tantus*, "high jingo" come again'. It may be, perhaps, that 'high tossing and swaggering preaching' gets them more prestige with the country people than if they talked homely good sense (a good point), but 'the main thing, I say, that makes many sermons so ridiculous . . . is *the inconsiderate use of frightful metaphors*'. Eachard's examples show that many of the Clergy have still not much altered their form.

Finally, he says — showing the modernity of his mind — all these old-fashioned Latin jokes and scholastic sophistries are hopelessly out of date. 'We are now in an age of Great Philosophers and Men of Reason.' Like Seth Ward and his circle, he realized the promise of the creative century in which he lived.[1] His criticism of Hobbes, unlike Lucy's, was likely to be up to date.

The other handicap from which the Clergy suffer is poverty. How can a man do himself justice if he is preoccupied with anxiety? With 'whose sow hath lately pigged and whence comes the next rejoicing goose?' Eachard paints a shocking and convincing picture of the straits to which many of the country Clergy were reduced, and insists on the need for better stipends.

Here, obviously, both in the field of University education and in everyday life, is a man of sound common sense, of humour and of principle. Rather a Philistine, perhaps, but benevolent. Not content to enjoy his own comparative prosperity, but a reformer. Rather a rare bird, probably in some Cambridge colleges in the middle decades of the seventeenth century.

Such was the mind brought to bear on Hobbes. Eachard was to contribute a new and more modern

---

[1] See Dr. V. Harris's curious book *All Coherence Gone*, C.U.P. (1949), which anatomizes the pessimism of the early seventeenth century in contrast to the new outlook.

element to the counter-attack under consideration.[1]
The first *Dialogue* (*Mr. Hobbes state of Nature considered in a Dialogue between Philautus and Timothy*) is
dedicated to Archbishop Sheldon, a steadfast patron of the
author.[2] It at once strikes the note that Hobbes has
disparaged human nature and must be refuted in popular
form. 'The same Divine Providence', writes Eachard,
'that hath made your Grace father of the Church hath
made you also guardian of Humane nature, which, as
your Grace well knows, has been so vilely aspersed and
persecuted by our adversaries malicious suggestions, that
he is unwilling to suffer such a word as man still to remain
among us, but what was always meant and designed
thereby he hath endeavoured to chase quite out of the
world. . . .'

'Mr. Hobbes,' he continues, 'by a starched mathematical method, by magisterial haughtiness . . . and the like
hath cheated some people into a vast opinion of himself . . .'
Actually, his writings are so 'fond and extravagant' as to
merit confutation in the light form of a dialogue. For
Hobbes' state of nature, he argues, implies 'a certain
supposed time, in which it was just and lawful for every
man to hang, draw and quarter, whom he pleased, when
he pleased, and after what manner he pleased; and to get,
possess, use and enjoy whatever he had a mind to . . .

---

[1] Clearly Swift's criticism of Eachard, quoted in the *Dictionary of National Biography*, was quite unjustified. 'I have known men happy enough at ridicule,' he wrote, 'who upon great subjects, were perfectly stupid, of which Dr. Eachard of Cambridge that writ the *Contempt of the Clergy* was a great instance.' The attack on Hobbes will further demonstrate that Eachard was no fool, but a man of sound judgment and penetrating mind.

[2] Eachard is mentioned in Anthony Wood's Autobiography. He was present when Wood was taken to dine with the Archbishop by Sir Leoline Jenkyns. Wood characteristically boasts that while he was taken into Sheldon's private room after dinner, Eachard was left to sit with the chaplains.

Neither could they be restrained by any Humane Laws because the Magistrate was not yet chosen'. But Hobbes is not really original. 'Neither is Human Nature (or reason) so very vile and raskally as he writes his own to be, nor his account altogether so demonstrative, as Euclid.'

The Dialogue opens briskly.

TIMOTHEUS Well met, Philautus, how does your best self this morning? What, stout and hearty? . . . Shall we take a turn or two in the Walks?

PHILAUTUS [Hobbes] No, I thank you, unless I know your tricks better; you may chance to get behind me, and bite me in the Legs.' He has been searching 'into the fundamental laws of humane nature' and 'knows better'.

Philautus is eventually persuaded to take a short turn. Timotheus inquires whether he has been 'affronted, abused, choused, defamed, flung down stairs, tossed in a blanket?'

PHIL. I'le assure thee Tim, I have always kept (as they say) out of harm's way, . . . especially since I studied morals . . . Then as a secret, Tim, I must tell thee, that men are naturally all ravenous and currish, of a very snarling and biting nature. To be short, they are in themselves mere Wolves, Tygers and Centaures.'

Timotheus admits that an egoist will be apt, when speaking of Commonwealth, 'to consult too much his own sweet elephants tooth', but accuses Philautus of devising 'little slender philosophical pretences to be wicked'.

PHIL. My works have sold very well.
TIM. They are but 'common acknowledged things new phrased'.

139

So they sit down on a bench to talk it out.

TIM. But hold, Sir, we ought to look under the bench
. . . there may lie a wolf that may quite spoil us.
PHIL. Say you so?
TIM. Come, come, Sir, no hurt at all . . . I had only a
mind to see how nimble you were.
PHIL. You Timothy sauce-boxe. . . .

Such is the very different atmosphere, all too rare in the
discussion of the heavier problems of political thought,
which Eachard is careful to create.

Philautus then arrogantly explains 'how . . . the morals
and politicks that have been written since the creation (as
they call it) of the world, were not worth a rush, till I set
forth mine'.[1] Here, in another idiom, is the old argument,
that Hobbes in his conceit is attempting to discard the
wisdom and knowledge of the past and setting himself
up to give the complete answer to all the greatest problems
of life, which was precisely what he was attempting to do.

Eachard proceeds to laugh at the title of Hobbes' earlier
book.

PHIL. 'Tis called 'Humane Nature, or the Fundamentals of Policie'.
TIM. . . . You might have called it as well *Tu quoque*,
or the Jealous Lovers, or the Fundamental Lawes of
Catching Quailes.

This mockery is too much for Hobbes.

Did you not promise me to be modest and not to prate?
Goe now and looke in the glasse.
TIM. Why — have you discoursed me into a *Bear*?

Anyway, continues Tim, there is nothing new in the

[1] p. 32.

book, 'save some small matter that was shirked up in
France from some of Cartes' acquaintances and spoiled in
the telling'. The Cartesian flavour of Hobbes' method
in spite of metaphysical differences, was plain enough to
his contemporaries.

Hobbes counters by saying that Timothy ignores his
main argument.

PHIL. But where's the state of war all this while? That's
the thing I long to be at, Tim; and to show thee for a
Fish.[1] [And, he continues], if I don't show thee for a fish,
I'le show thee to be a Beast, and all mankind besides.'

But mankind, objects Tim: is 'tolerably tame . . . methinks
it is a great pity now at last to be sent to the Tower
amongst the Lyons'. For Hobbes, man is an 'arrant
wolfe', but civil society is not what Hobbes depicts it to
be. 'When I heard this I expected the whole world
naturally to be all in armes and an uproare, tearing and
worrying one another like mad . . . and to hear nothing
but "down with him there!" "Hang him with his own
gutts" . . . Split him down the chine, or roaste him with
a couple of awles in his eyes!'

Actually, he says, society is much more civilized — a
state of affairs incompatible with Hobbes' assumptions.
But Philautus cites the quarrelsomeness of children, and
Timotheus mocks him in the remark about the 'little
state of nature', previously quoted.[2]

Eachard now proceeds to depict a specimen island,
which he calls the *Isle of Pines*. Here, 'so we start fair'
let us assume it 'rains men' — 'Not a mere Scotch mist of
babies.' We assume, he says, 'four well complexioned up-

<hr>

[2] See above, p. 32.

right gents, about fifteen hands high, which shall happen, in a shower of rain, to fall upon an island of four hundred acres, viz. the Isle of Pines'.[1] They are called *Dick*, *Roger*, *Tumbler* and *Towser*. It is absurd, says Timotheus, to assume they will fall out. 'Must they needs set up their tails and fall a-snarling?'

They must, Philautus objects, for they are in a state of war, since there has been no covenant made.

TIM. That's right. Unless they happened (as they came tumbling down), to call in at old Jones of Upper Enfield and there cracked a pot and shaked hands.

The assumption, Timotheus insists, is absurd. According to Philautus, 'Four honest rogues come to earth, falling either upon several places of the island, or being in a great mist, or coming before daylight.' They are unknown to one another, and therefore have not spoken. It follows, he says, that they are in a state of war. What nonsense! If this be a sample of the state of nature, it is plainly absurd. A ridiculous example of the state of nature, objects Philautus. But Timotheus insists that his argument stands or falls by whether the four men on the island collaborate or not. 'If humane nature, upon first view, pricks up its ears and sets up its scut and falls presently

---

[1] It is likely that the name was taken from a widely read book pseudonymously written four years before by Henry Neville (1620-94), author of *Plato Redivivus* and editor of Machiavelli. (He was a member of the Rota Club and an associate of Harrington.) This pamphlet, which had a wide success, was entitled *The Isle of Pines, discovered near to the coast of Terra Australis Incognita by Henry van Sloetten, in a letter to his friend in London, declaring the Truth of his voyage to the East Indies*. London, 1668. 'When this was first published,' says an inscription in a contemporary hand in the copy in the Bodleian Library, "Twas looked upon as a sham.' It purports to give an account of a Commonwealth in the Indian Ocean. Here the inhabitants are descended from an Elizabethan sailor, George Pine, three white women and a negress. ('I gave these people the name of the "English Pines".') Neville also wrote various coarse parodies, one called *News from the New Exchange, or the Commonwealth of Ladies* (London, printed in the year of women without grace, 1650).

to tearing and slicing and slashing, then the battle goes to your side.' If, on the other hand, they behave sensibly; if they 'Treat', and live in peace, 'the Day is Mine'.

To this Philautus replies that if they come to an arrangement it will only be through fear, and Eachard paraphrases Hobbes remarks about the certain 'market fellowship' which is all that is begotten when men come together. But, Timotheus insists, to deny that 'market fellowship' is sociability is absurd; there is, of course, advantage in it, but that is not all. If the motive was merely fear, society would present a very different appearance: of apprehension rather than vitality. Mankind would be habitually cowed. 'They would huddle together like a brood of ducklings for mutual consolation, and get close into a corner with head under wing, and make not the least noise for fear of waking original sin.' On the contrary, human societies show enterprise and optimism. Society, argues Timotheus, is spontaneous, not the result of deliberate calculation. But Philautus continues to argue: fear is its inspiration — mutual fear is 'a naturall . . . and deeply seated . . . taint'.[1] Look at kings, he says, with their forts and drawbridges and guns. That, counters Tim, echoing Lucy and Lawson, is merely because a minority make these things necessary, internally and externally. It does not follow that because you have constables and watches that all men are bad. There is a minority of criminals and madmen — 'Fifth monarchy men and Quakers' (then regarded as dangerous) whose 'religious frenzy may disturb the peace'. Or you may get drunkards — a real menace in days when men went about armed — or a 'wild boar or an ox'. Or thieves, 'who think it a piece of dull pedantry to live by any profession'. But to 'conclude from this that humane nature is a "shirking, rooking, pilfering padding nature", is as extravagant as to say that the 'true state of nature is perpetual drunkenness'.

Nor are the great conquerors and warriors representative of ordinary human nature. 'Because Alexander had a mind to try an experiment and see how much mischief he could do in his whole life time; or because the Caesars spoiled many Kingdoms, or because the Turk gave twopence for a pigeon to tell him from above that the whole earth was his', it does not follow such behaviour is common. Eachard has no use for the glamour of conquest. This English way of regarding military adventurers as a nuisance is most salutary. It is a pity it so seldom took on abroad.

As for Philautus, he can do what he likes — take elaborate and grotesque precautions for his personal safety — but such conduct does not apply to the general run of humanity. 'Do what you like for yourself. Ride with eight suspecting pistols, a half dozen heeding swords: let a file of anticipating musketeers walk constantly before you — and as many subjugating ones behind. Plant a defending blunderbuss upon the top of your stairs, put on a head-piece instead of a quilted cap and sleep in perfect armour . . . and if a mouse comes, cry out that the Turke is landed.'[1] But don't imagine that proves your case. It will merely prove your eccentricity.

Having thus pointed out in good plain terms one of the more obvious absurdities of this aspect of Hobbes' argument, Timotheus takes him up on a fundamental

[1] 'The Grand Turke' is constantly in their minds: compare Stalin today. See below, Clarendon, p. 166, Whitehall, p. 180.

metaphysical point with which we have been frequently concerned.

Philautus denies the existence of right and wrong outside man-made societies. 'Only metaphysical term-drivers talk about intrinsic right and wrong — good and evil. They are all utterly besotted, there being no such being at all but what the magistrate may please to appoint.' Further, says this radical sceptic, there can be no property rights before covenant. The position is familiar.

Timotheus tries to show its absurdity by reverting to the four 'Pineyards'. 'They can't enjoy anything', says Philautus, 'Unless they agree formally first' . . . This is absurd, answers his opponent, 'to say they can't enjoy anything "before Jonas Moore" — (the surveyor) — has come to divide and call that piece "Starve Crowe", and 'tother "Long Acre", and because the white posts are not yet up by Roger's door and because Dick hath not determined what coat of arms to set upon his sheep's back.' Can you really pretend that there are no property rights until these things have been done? They can quite well take a share of a strip without exact legal division. Hobbes' argument, he insists, is artificial.

Philautus, not well able to answer, becomes annoyed. 'I pray thee go home and put thy head into a pipkin, and there stewe it till thou gettest more wit . . . I have considered and weighed, as young Toys as thou art never do.' (Timotheus is cast as a young man, to appeal to the audience Eachard had in mind.)

Returning to the four 'Pineyards', Timotheus takes up Hobbes on another well-known argument — that men are equal in the capacity to kill.

But they will not be so equal. 'Roger may chance to

have a huge legg, Dick the quicker eyes, Tumbler the bigger fist, Towser the better breath and longer nailes.'

Turning to the wider theme of natural rights, Timotheus argues that Governments have no right to irresponsible power. 'There be several things most firmly and undoubtedly good in themselves, and will continue to be so, let all the supremes' (Powers) 'in the world meet together to vote them down.' And there be others that are so obviously bad, that 'all the princes on earth cannot given them credit'.

This argument, that we know decency and fair play and workable political methods when we see them (as a farmer, says Cicero, knows the virtues of a good horse)[1] is a strong 'intuitional' basis for rejecting Hobbes' assumptions. Here is a theme at once echoing tradition and anticipating eighteenth-century arguments for Rational Theology and morals. Moreover, says Timotheus, the magistrate needn't grumble because during the 'vacation', which was the state of nature, certain things were obviously good and bad. Such reinforcement helps government. In conclusion, he declares that you cannot 'call a council of two or three or of nineteen, or mount all the cannons in the tower, against the next Spring Tide'. The existence of these values must be accepted. But Philautus remains obstinately unconvinced. 'Very fine things,' he says, 'these goods and bads.' If the magistrate didn't make them, who did?

Having thus debated several major points raised by the 'Pineyards' descent on their island, Philautus and Timothy decide to go to luncheon. 'It begins,' says Timotheus, 'to be time to think of some protection for

[1] *de legibus*, i, 16.

that inward member of the body, called the stomach.' 'In that, Tim, I agree with thee,' answers his antagonist, 'but in nothing else.'

Such are some of the brisk debating points set out in the first *Dialogue*. By reducing the statements of Hobbes to their practical implications and depicting the absurdities implied, Eachard has done much to clarify the questions raised, despite the trenchant words, fine writing and debating skill whereby Hobbes clothes his ideas with prestige. Commonplace, racy and homely, much of this shrewd criticism is difficult to answer. It certainly brings out clearly the questions involved.

The Second Dialogue, written in 1673 (*Some Opinions of Mr. Hobbes considered in a Second Dialogue between Philautus and Timothy*) carries out the technique more thoroughly and on a larger scale.[1]

After an apology to Archbishop Sheldon ('I must humbly beg your grace's pardon if I have endeavoured to smile a little and get as much out of his road and way of writing as possible') Eachard proceeds to a high-spirited parody of a bookseller's 'puff'. He cannot, says the bookseller, compete with Hobbes in self-advertisement. 'But, however, reader do so much as hold my hatt and gloves, and thou shall see what such an unprejudiced person can do for a poor modest, shiftless, friendless, despairing, dying author.'

'Dost thou want, reader,' the bookseller proceeds, 'a just, true, and impartial History of the whole World? ... trouble not thy self, here 'tis. It begins ten thousand years before the oldest Pre-Adamite, and holds good and first

[1] Printed by J. Macock for Walter Kettilby at the sign of the Bishops-head in St. Pauls Churchyard, 1673. (Reprinted for T. Davies, 1783.)

ten thousand years after the world shall end. Dost thou want . . . Divinity? . . . This book was at the first four General Councils and in all the Persecutions. Hast thou a mind to a compleat body of Law? . . . The twelve Tables were stolen out of the book last week, when it was printing.'

Perhaps the reader is ignorant of medicine? 'Dost thou want Galen, Hippocrates, Paracelsus, etc.? want thou still; for in effect thou hast them all.' The book, indeed, is infallible for all technical purposes.

'Dost thou want a Book to measure the height of the stars, survey Ground, make a Dial, &c.? Look pag 79 lin. 12. it tells thee exactly what's a Clock, either by day or by night.' It will, further, serve as an alarm clock. 'Turn down the fourth leaf of this Book when thou goest to bed and 'twill go off just at that hour.'

'It doubles, Cubes and Squares, (better than Mr. Hobbes,) only with an Oyster shell and a pair of Tobacco Tongs.' And if you 'chomp three or four lines of it in a morning; it scours and clarifies the Teeth'.

Moreover, it is a very accomplished book. 'It does not only sing, dance, play on the Lute, speak French, ride the great Horse, &c.,' but it performs all family duties. 'It runs for a Midwife: it rocks the Cradle, combs the Childs head, sweeps the House, milks the Cows, turns the Hogs out of the Corn, . . . all this it doth at the same time, and yet is never out of breath.'

Its popularity abroad is immense.

'Never was any book more magnified beyond the seas.' The foreigners are all talking about it. 'Go into France, Spain, Italy, or any other part of Europe, — no other discourse but of the Dutch war and of the *Second Dialogue*.'

It has had a beneficial effect on international politics. 'If the French and the King of Brandenburge have agreed, without doubt 'twas done by this *Second Dialogue*. And if ever we beat the Dutch 'twill be just after the same manner as Tim hath slain the Leviathan. For 'tis already translated into Latin, Greek, French, Spanish and the Universal language.'

Cicero prophesied of it.

'Alluding to this *Dialogue*,' he says, *omnes ex omni aetate libri, si unum in locum conferentur, cum Servio Sulpitio Timotheo, non sunt conferendi*. ' 'Tis needless to say what Xenophon, Josephus, Varro and the Talmud say of it.'

It has one added advantage. There is no need, of course, actually to read it. 'But now, Reader, I take leave — but only to let you know that I am very doubtful whether this book is worth reading. But if you understand me aright, 'tis the more valuable for that. For such is the vertue of this book that the meer buying of it will do all the feats above-mentioned.' 'And, therefore,' he concludes, 'lay down your money: and so farewell?'

After this spirited beginning, Eachard addresses the public, taking a line rather similar to the authors of *1066 and All That*, whose object, it will be remembered, was to console the reader.

"Tis not the design of the following Dialogue, neither was it of the former, to make sport for idle people . . . but to preserve thee from being laughed at.'

So Eachard next proceeds to analyse the three types who admire Hobbes; the naturally wicked; the silly fashionable young men, and the old pompous academics.

At the same time, he insists, his purpose is serious. 'I have not spent my time so very ill as to collect a few tales and proverbs to make others merry. Nor was it writ either to please the Churchmen — whose office, power and Bible Mr. Hobbes cunningly hath disposed of — nor to oblige the Lords and Commons, who may stay at home, if the Prince take his advice — but, if it were possible, to cure a company of easy, giddy, small-pated gentlemen who swagger that Mr. Hobbes hath said more for a bad life and against the other life after this, than ever was pleaded by philosophers or divines to the contrary.' To effect this cure is ten times more difficult than to answer all Mr. Hobbes' works.

The first of the three types that read him are 'the sturdy resolved practitioners in Hobbesianism, and most certainly would have been so had there never been such a man as Mr. Hobbes in the world. But when they heard that ill nature, debauching and irreligion were mathematical and demonstrative', and that Hobbes was a 'very observing gent, and yet writ as viciously and prophanely as their own vanity and lusts could tempt them to practice', then they had found a philosopher exactly to their purpose. These are his 'constant Pit friends'.

The next kind are frivolous young men, anxious to appear worldly and cynical. 'The next school that came into Mr. Hobbes are a sort of small, soft, little pretty fine gents, who having some little witt, some little modesty, some little remains of conscience and country religion, could not tear and hector it as the former, but quickly learnt to chirp and giggle when the other clapt and shouted. And these are Mr. Hobbes' gallery friends.'

The third kind are the portentous scholars, and intellectual snobs. They are the solemn, the judicious, the 'Don-Admirers'. They are 'the Box friends of Mr. Hobbes'.

'Being men of gravity and reputation . . . they will scarce simper in favour of the philosopher, but can make shift to nod and nod again, and think no man but Mr. Hobbes has gone to the fundamentals of government or human nature.'

For the first, says Eachard, they are past cure; the second type is his target — to them the book is mainly directed. As to the third, let them reflect on the consequences of Hobbes' ideas. He puts the Prince above all religion — uncomfortable doctrine for the Clergy — and cuts right across the country's institutions. 'Having given him such a full brimmer of Power . . . as to be sure he hath raised him above our Form of Government.' Yet, subversive as he is of the native tradition, 'This his prince you take for a rare Prince, and these his Politicks for rare Politicks . . .' Yet, if you reflect, you will find there is nothing really new in his Commonwealth, 'only saucy impudent reflections upon the Laws, Constitutions, and Government of our Realm'. Hobbes, he insists, like the other critics here examined, undermines the predominant political tradition of his country.

Further, he argues, 'don't mistake yourselves — he's every whit as much against civil power as ecclesiastical' and clean against the custom of the realm. Why even the King 'likes such money as is given him by Parliament — and such Laws as they advise him to make' — and 'He thinks himself Prince enough and is contented with his place', though he can't live up to Hobbes' idea of him, or 'turn God out of the world'.

Actually, all Hobbes is fit for is to be a 'very good English Grammarian'. He would have made 'a most absolute, unlimited, irresistable sovereign of a country school, and upon play days we'll allow him to translate. He has done Thucydides well'. For when you come to grips with his argument and 'pull his phrases a-pieces' you find it poor stuff. 'I have always found that to confute him thoroughly you have only to understand him aright.' As for the rest of his politics, they are known to every dragoon.

With this insistence on the pretentiousness of Hobbes and the significant assumption, common to the other critics, that his principles subvert 'our' constitution — Eachard ends his preface and proceeds to his main argument, of which only a very summary impression can be given here.

After some skirmishing about metaphysical questions, Eachard refers to Hobbes' controversy with Bramhall. Philautus remarks, 'I was forced to let him know that his lordship writes like a beast, nay worse than a beast, both in sense and cleanliness . . . and as for his language 'tis jargon — Tohu Bohu.' To which Timotheus comments, sardonically, ''Twas a most unhappy thing that so great a churchman should run himself into such danger.' The *Dialogue* continues for some time on the question of liberty and freewill, not directly concerned with politics. Timotheus presses Hobbes hard, saying that if men are automata, then God is responsible for sin — Hobbes, in fact, is a Manichee, a point noticed before.[1] He proceeds to attack Hobbes for pomposity, and makes some shrewd hits at Hobbes' 'Magisterial' style.

Take, for example, a simple thought — 'If we here in our country have more pudding than plumbs and other people have more plumbs than pudding, the best way will

[1] See above, Rosse, p. 63.

be for the pudding and plumbs to hold a correspondence.'

This is Hobbes' version, 'And because there is no territory under Dominion of the Commonwealth, except it be of vast extent, that produceth all things needful for the maintenance, and motion of the whole body; and few that produce not something more than necessary; the superfluous commodities to be had within, become no more superfluous, but supply these wants at home by importation of that which may be had abroad, either by exchange, or by just war, or by labour.'[1] Now this is typical — and it sounds very fine. But what beyond Eachard's simple idea, do the words amount to? 'They are magnificently and flaringly dressed up.' He further laughs at Hobbes' pomposity over the exchange of labour, a way of expression which has contributed to the jargon of modern economics.

'Suppose a man profers his dog Jowler a good large piece of bread on condition that he skips cleverly over his stick. Here is a tacite kind of promise, a dog's labour being a commodity exchangeable for benefit . . .', though Jowler wasn't able to say 'Done Master'.

The remainder of the *Dialogue* is concerned with an attempt to confute Hobbes out of his own mouth, and with ridiculing Hobbes' portentous manner of expression. He cites Hobbes' remarks about the brute creation compared with human societies, which occur in the *De Cive* and are repeated in the *Leviathan*. 'Their Government', says Hobbes, 'is not "politic" because it is only by consent of many wills concerned in one object, not, as is necessary in civil government, one will.'

How comes it about, asks Eachard, that 'Bees live con-

[1] *Leviathan*, chap. xxiv, par. 4.

tentedly without chusing one supreme unlimited Buzzer, or one assembly of Bees, that by plurality of Buzzers may be brought to consent in one Buzz'. There is 'no contestation for honour among Bees'. 'If one Bee has a mind to be made Burgess or Knight of the Shire, "March on", say the rest. "Honey is a very good thing" ' — an admirable phrase.

Eachard continues to quote Hobbes' elaborate and laboriously worked out metaphors about the body politic: the comparison of the community to a gigantic man, with his various parts represented by some aspect of society; the comparison of commerce to the circulation of the blood and the remarks on the nutrition and procreation of Commonwealths in the twenty-fourth chapter of the *Leviathan*. Yet, says Eachard, Hobbes, in the earlier part of the work, complains of 'metaphors, Tropes and other rhetorical figures' as the 'cause of very absurd conclusions'. And he cites Hobbes' assertion that 'the light of humane minds is perspicuous words' and that 'metaphors are *ignes fatui*'. Yet, concludes Eachard, 'Philautus himself can smack his lips over an anchovy'.

As for Hobbes' passion for mathematics, it must now be diminished since his controversy with Dr. Wallis, though he got much advertisement by it. Once he 'slabbered over his dear Mis, his sweet and honey mathematicks', but 'poor Aurelia is now grown old'.

The book proceeds to a final scene in which the implications of Hobbes' religious ideas are worked out. He is represented as being forced to deny God and Christ by an absolute Prince.

Relentlessly the scene develops, as Hobbes is hailed before the ruler and forced from one position to a worse one. Philautus attempts to stave off the conclusion. 'But, if after that, Philautus, his Lieutenant cocks his hat, stamps, looks big, and says he is sure — he is very *sure*, that there is nothing (either in heaven or earth) that is better or greater than he himself, and that you shall be sure of it, too, before he and you part' — what shall Philautus do now?

The dialogue proceeds, like the conversation between a bully and his victim at school. At each stroke Timothy makes an encouraging remark.

'Well done, Carcass, thus have we turned off . . . God the Father. Now let us see how we can get rid of Christ or God the Son.' And when it comes to that too, 'Rarely come off, Carcass again!' The dialogue concludes with an attack on Hobbes for undermining the belief in Hell.

The contribution of Dr. John Eachard to the criticism of Hobbes is certainly original and formidable.

In conclusion the opinion of the editor of his reprinted works is worth quotation. In the easy English of the late eighteenth century he writes: 'In this [*The Second Dialogue*] he has employed all the powers of his wit to expose the false reasoning and specious sophistry of the Philosopher of Malmesbury. And surely the gravest reader cannot help being highly diverted with the happy strokes of fine humour and keen raillery with which he has attacked and entirely confuted the absurd and dogmatical lectures of this inveterate enemy of true religion and sound morals.' 'All the serious and systematical books, written by the most eminent and learned of our divines could never have rendered the philosophy of Hobbes so contemptible as the incomparable dialogues of Eachard, which contain the most judicious arguments, united with the most spirited satire and the liveliest mirth.'

Further, he continues, 'Eachard had, besides a vein of humour peculiar to himself, much useful learning, a strong manner of reasoning, without the appearance of it, and above all an uncommon skill in turning an adversary into ridicule; in which no writer has since exceeded nor perhaps equalled him. Let us not forget, too, that he possessed an inexhaustible fund of good nature which the haughty and splenetical Swift could never enjoy.'

Finally, the editor remarks, Dryden thought very highly of the *Dialogues*. 'The way which Lucian chose of delivering these profitable and pleasing truths was that of the Dialogue. A choice worthy of the Author, happily followed by Erasmus and Fontenelle particularly, to whom I may justly add a triumvir of our own, the Reverend, ingenious and learned Dr. Eachard, who by using the same method, the same ingredients of raillery and reason, has more baffled the philosopher of Malmesbury, than those who assaulted him with the blunt heavy arguments drawn from orthodox divinity: for Hobbes foresaw where these strokes would fall, and leapt aside before they could descend; but he could not avoid those nimble passes which were made on him, by a wit more active than his own, and which were within his body before he could provide for his defence.'

There seems much to be said for both these opinions after a reading of the two *Dialogues* of Dr. Eachard, that Bellocian don, whose boisterous epigrams and rapier wit contributed to the controversy not only a political polemic but a curiosity of literature.

CHAPTER VIII

CLARENDON'S *BRIEF VIEW OF THE DANGEROUS AND PERNICIOUS ERRORS OF MR. HOBBES HIS LEVIATHAN*

'WHATEVER errors may have been brought into the world by Aristotle, no man ever grew a rebel by reading him.' Clarendon's opinion strikes a conservative note. Here is the voice of a statesman who, for seven years, has held great power; of an experienced politician who looks upon the consequences of Hobbes' ideas for government.

His point of view is rare among writers on political theory. In general, great ministers of State are too busy making history to theorize about politics, and if they record their opinions tend to write memoirs or narrative. In this context Clarendon is here in a class by himself. The previous contributors to the common offensive have been academic, and only one of them, Bramhall, had wielded power in the great world. Clarendon speaks, and speaks alone, for the point of view of government; and like Whitehall, he speaks as a lawyer.

In another aspect he is also representative. Edward Hyde is typical of his class; none of the other critics, save Bramhall, belonged to it. He was not only a great magnate; he had risen from just that level of the country gentry from whom the upper ranks of the growing bureaucracy were drawn in the middle seventeenth century; from a class whose achievements were to be the most constructive legacy of the age.

Here brought to bear on Hobbes, is the point of view of a statesman, and also of a country gentleman who had made his way by the law — typical of the most responsible and the ablest section of the country at that time.

The background of Clarendon's family is worth a moment's consideration. It is revealed in his autobiography, surely one of the most attractive of the many memoirs which have come down from a period rich in such records. It partly explains his point of view.

The Hydes came originally from Norbury near Chester, but Clarendon's grandfather, Laurence Hyde, had settled in Wiltshire. He had worked in the office of the auditor of the Exchequer, and had been employed in a similar capacity by Sir John Thynne at Longleat. He had made a judicious marriage to Anne Colthurst, relict of Matthew Colthurst, a landowner of Claverton near Bath, and with her dowry he bought West Hatch, near Tisbury, about fourteen miles west of Salisbury on the way to Shaftesbury — a small and methodical beginning. Laurence Hyde had four sons and two daughters. The eldest, Robert, inherited the West Hatch estate. Lawrence, the next, became Attorney General to Queen Anne, the Danish Consort of James I. The third son, Henry, was Clarendon's father. The fourth son, Nicholas, became Lord Chief Justice of the King's Bench. Of his two daughters, Joan married into the family of Young of Durnford; they were to be a well-known royalist Wiltshire family, connected by marriage with Colonel Penruddock of the rebellion. The other, Ann, married into the Baynard family of Wanstrow, Somerset, of whom a branch had property at Tincleton in Dorset, near Dorchester. The family displayed a notable solidarity. All the Hyde brothers were educated at Oxford. By worldly standards, Clarendon's father, Henry, was the least successful. But he had inherited the lease of the impropriate rectory of Dinton, near Tisbury; he had made a good marriage with Mary Langford of Trowbridge, and he lived at Dinton 'with great cheerfulness, content and integrity'. He had been a burgess to Parliament in the last years of Elizabeth, but never afterwards went to London. Clarendon's mother had never been there.

In 1622, Edward was sent to Oxford. He was a year at Magdalen Hall, the same foundation that had educated Hobbes, and was elected a demy of Magdalen College in the next year. In 1625, at sixteen, he proceeded to the Middle Temple, with the patronage of his uncle, Nicholas Hyde. After building up a successful practice at the Law, he entered Parliament as member for Wootton Bassett in north Wiltshire in 1640.

This background is worth attention; it is representative and explains his point of view. With all that world — collectively the most influential in England[1] — the nephew of the Malmesbury clothier had little in common. With it his theories would cut little ice. Here is a close family interest and co-operation, characteristic of the rising gentry, with their roots in their country properties and in Oxford, their links with the professional world in London, with their responsibility for local government. It is typical of a world far too practical and shrewd to set much store by Hobbes' theoretical dogmatism, whatever

[1] Contemptuously described by Marxist historians by the contradictory term 'the rural bourgeoisie'.

its originality and power in the field of philosophy. Of course these people were apt to be complacent and insular. 'In 1639', Clarendon remarks, 'England enjoyed the greatest measure of felicity that it had ever known ... the two crowns of France and Spain worrying each other ... and all Germany weltering in its own blood.' This complacency and conservatism is reflected in the attack on Hobbes. Here Clarendon reveals a very old-fashioned outlook — much more of the 'right' than Lawson, for example. As historians generally agree, Clarendon, like Filmer, held to a belated Tudor paternalism. He not only objects to Hobbes' utilitarian and sceptical assumptions, but he denies that power is derivative from contract. Rather it is innate in the King and only modified by 'condescent of grace'. The function of Parliaments is consultative and they need only be called at the King's will, says this House of Commons lawyer, surprisingly.

Although he objects to the Whig argument, Clarendon has no use for Hobbes.[1] He was smarting under the bitterness of exile, but his allegiance to Charles, he insists, is unimpaired. 'It is one of the false and evil Doctrines which Mr. *Hobbes* hath published . . . *That a banished Subject, during the banishment, is not a subject . . . and that a banish'd man is a lawful Enemy of the Common-wealth that*

---

[1] His book is entitled *A Brief View and Survey of the Dangerous and pernicious Errors to Church and State, in Mr. Hobbes' Book, Entitled LEVIATHAN. By Edward Earl of Clarendon . . . Oxon. Printed at the Theater* 1676. The dedication to Charles II was written at Moulins on the Loire, and dated May 10th, 1673. There follows a preface and survey of Hobbes' introduction. The main text, *A Survey of Mr. Hobbbes His Leviathan*, runs to 322 pages. He follows the argument of the Leviathan closely, chapter by chapter, devoting from pages 16 to 194 to the first thirty-one chapters of Hobbes; pages 195 to 284 to part III of the *Leviathan*, and pages 285 to 322 to part IV. He is not, therefore, like some of the other critics, primarily concerned with religion.

The book is well produced, with a frontispiece of Andromeda, a figure of Rubensesque proportions, with her chains broken, standing against a rock; above, on a winged horse, Perseus flourishes Medusa's head. Beneath him is a Leviathan, spouting foam.

banish'd him.' 'I thank God,' he continues, 'from the time I found myself under the insupportable burden of Your Majestie's displeasure and under the infamous brand of Banishment, I have not felt myself one minute absolved in the least degree from the obligation of the strictest duty to your person.'

He can now think of nothing better worth doing (next to writing his History of the Rebellion) than to confute Hobbes, a writer pernicious to Kings and destructive of allegiance. He has often tried to warn Charles II against Hobbes, and even to persuade the King (evidently without effect) to give himself the 'leisure and the trouble' to read the *Leviathan*, thus depriving Hobbes' epigrams of their 'pithy prestige' out of context. He dwells on his own difficulties in being cut off from books and critics, but he concludes that he still 'assumes the title of . . . faithful and obedient Subject' . . . 'one of the oldest servants now living to your Father and your Self', he says, with a sting of reproach. He can still confute this 'book of great name'; one which 'contains in it good learning of all kinds politely extracted and very wittily and cunningly digested and in a vigorous and pleasant style'. But Hobbes is too introspective. His friends say he spends too much time in turning over his own notions and too little in discussion. Moreover 'his natural constitution, with age, contracted such a morosity that contradicting men were never grateful to him'.

The dons, he proceeds, have been slow to answer him. 'I did suppose some University men to have vindicated those venerable nurseries from that vice and ignorance his superciliousness hath thought to asperse them with.' All they have done is to attack his geometry — a course which had the effect of annoying him more than any other. It is curious, in view of the chorus of criticism which had assailed Hobbes, of which only some of the best political specimens have been examined, that Clarendon took this line. Too busy to attend to the earlier controversy, he would not, one feels, have approved of Eachard's *Dialogues* which had appeared since his exile. He is, himself, well qualified to criticize Hobbes' political doctrines, he declares, having acted his part for many years in the administration of Justice and in the 'policy of the Kingdom'. He feels, therefore, 'that this leisure to which God hath condemned me, seems an obligation'.

Making the same point as Eachard, he says that Hobbes' style disguises the poverty and perniciousness of his conclusions. There are 'Too many people who, pleased with his *style*, have not taken notice of those downright conclusions which overthrow and undermine all those principles of Government which have preserved the Peace of this Kingdom through so many ages.'

Turning to a personal anecdote, Clarendon relates how when he was in Jersey he heard that Mr. Hobbes was in Paris at the time of the publication of his *De Cive*. He sent to Hobbes for a copy and informed him that Sidney Godolphin had left Hobbes £200. Clarendon told him to get in touch with Francis Godolphin who would pay the legacy. And that was why Hobbes dedicated his *Leviathan* to Francis Godolphin, whom he had never seen. When, later, they met in Paris, Hobbes told him how Godolphin had paid down £100 and promised the rest. Hobbes thanked Clarendon, but warned him he would not like his *Leviathan*. 'The truth is,' he had said, 'I have a mind to go home.'

Against this accusation must be set Hobbes' denial. 'What was Oliver when the book came forth?'

When the book arrived in Flanders — and Hobbes had presented 'a copy engraved in vellum, in a marvellous fair hand, to the King' (as Clarendon implies, he never bothered to read it), Clarendon read it with interest. But he could never understand why Hobbes, who had such an admiration for Government, should write a book for which 'any constituted Government in Europe must arrest him'. This view was confirmed. The French authorities threatened to apprehend him — one of the reasons of his return to England.

After this significant anecdote, Clarendon continues the survey of Hobbes' introduction. Hobbes starts with a false assumption that men are rational. Anyone with political experience knows this to be untrue — 'We have,' says the old statesman, 'too much cause to believe that much the major part of mankind do not think at all.'

They have, he says, 'no reflection . . .' They are 'not endowed with reason enough to opine or think what they did last, or what they are to do next'. Moreover, men are profoundly different. 'They are not more unlike each other in their faces or in their clothes, than in their thinking, hoping and fearing.' Nor can we tell what is in their minds. 'As the fears, so the hopes of men are as unlike as their gait and mien.' 'If a sanguine and a melancholic man hope the same thing, their hopes are no more alike each others than their complections are.' Here are the conclusions of a man well versed in the world.

He proceeds to his main and fundamental argument, which is contained in the criticism of the chapters XIII-XVI. Hobbes' premises are all utterly wrong. 'Under the notion of explaining Common Terms', he dazzles men's eyes from discerning the fallacies upon which he raises his structure. His estimate of human nature — like that of most 'planners' — is an affront to human dignity. 'God did not make men lower than beasts.' It would be contrary to God's purpose 'that He should leave His creature, His masterpiece, in a war of all against all'. Why, animals, he says, following the other critics, do not prey on one another within the same species.

> — *Quando leoni*
> *Fortior eripuit vitam leo? quo nemore unquam*
> *Expiravit aper majoris dentibus apri?*

Yet, according to Hobbes, man, created in the likeness of God himself, is the only creature in the world that 'out of the indignity of his own nature, and the base fear that is inseparable from it, is obliged for his own benefit, and for the defence of his own rights, to worry and destroy all of his own kind, until they all become yoked by a covenant and contract that Mr. Hobbes hath provided for them, and which was never yet entered into by any one man, and is by nature impossible to be entered into'.

Further, Hobbes' examples are wrong-headed. Locking up houses, he says, and going armed, echoing Lucy and Lawson's argument, only implies 'wariness' against a minority of criminals. For 'if there be two or three Drunkards in a Town, all men have reason to go arm'd in the streets to controul the violence, or indignity they might receive from them'.[1]

Clarendon, further, strongly denounces the implications of Hobbes' suppression of free thought.

[1] p. 29.

'We need to watch Mr. Hobbes very carefully when the legislative fitt is uppon him, lest he cast such a net over us that we be deprived of both the use of our liberty and our reason to oppose him.' Seth Ward, now Bishop of Salisbury, had been of the same opinion in 1654.

As for Hobbes' false notion of the equality of men, which contradicts Aristotle, it is disproved by history — 'When we see a Marius, from a common soldier, baffle the nobility of Rome, and despite of opposition, make himself seven times Consul, or a Diocletian raise himself to the full state and power of the greatest Emperor; Marmurius, from a blacksmith become an Emperor . . .' And consider the great Tamberlaine. 'Neither his Climate nor his conversation' could account for it. All were self-made, and after their deaths their power collapsed. [1]

Hobbes' misinterpretation of the laws of nature and attempt to have it both ways are particularly reprehensible. 'How should it come to pass that Mr. Hobbes, while he is demolishing the whole frame of nature for want of order to support it, and makes it unavoidably necessary for every man to cut his neighbour's throat . . . in all of which there is no injustice . . . I say, how comes it to pass, that at the same time he is possessed of this frenzy, he should in the same, and in the next chapter, set down such a body of laws prescribed by nature itself as immutable and eternal?'

If these laws are valid, he asks, why the jungle conditions Hobbes dogmatically assumes? He arrogantly constitutes himself the 'plenipotentiary of nature'.

Proceeding to another fundamental aspect of the

Leviathan, Clarendon roundly denies that sovereigns have power from anyone but God. The 'Whig' argument, set out by Lawson and Hunton, he flatly contradicts. It is an innovating, rash, idea. *'That the power was divided between the King and the Lords and the House of Commons*, was an opinion never heard of in *England* till the Rebellion was begun.'[1] 'Condescent' there must be, whereby the King diminishes his power for the sake of smooth government, but it is by condescent only. This authority differs from Hobbes' absolutism, which 'would have such a power and authority as the Great Turke hath not yet appeared to affect'. Of course 'such a Commonwealth would be a much worse Commonwealth than ever was in the world': there is no government like this 'figment'. For government, though not 'elected', must depend on popular support — on public opinion, says Clarendon, with insight. Certainly the security, peace and happiness of the people is the end of government, but this can come about only by wise rule from above. Nowhere is Clarendon's 'belated Elizabethan' outlook better expressed.

Such an absolute power, he goes on, wisely, would be precarious. Even if Hobbes' covenant were real, the people have made it only between themselves, and posterity would not be bound by 'such an unthrifty concession of their parents'. They would call God's Lieutenant the 'Vizier Basha'. Doubtless Hobbes concocted this idea because he wanted to conciliate the rebel government. He wished to 'appear a courtier to the sovereign power that then governed, by how odious and horrible a usurpation soever'.[2]

[1] p. 54.   [2] See below, p. 181.

The King can have no truck with this new fangled and arbitrary power. His authority is securely based on a better foundation. For the King is no representative, but sovereign by descent of six hundred years. And the Parliament is only representative in so far as the King likes to call them and consult them. For Parliament is not Parliament save in conjunction with the King, and they are only representative in that they are petitioners. Here is the usual royalist doctrine with a clear medieval descent. He proceeds, in his criticisms of chapters XIX and XX, to elaborate it. For the King's Majesty is inherent in his office, and legally the King never dies. Clearly Hobbes' doctrine of succession was simply for the benefit of Cromwell's 'vile posterity'. For princes cannot nominate their successor: the succession goes by descent. Not even in Poland or the Holy Roman Empire or the Papacy — and that is not hereditary, 'since Caesar Borgia was so long since dead'.

Clarendon then embarks upon a long historical survey of 'dominion'. Peace not war is 'founded in nature'. After Adam, 130 years later, came Seth, lord of the world. 'Nor have we the least colour to believe that there was either sedition or civil war before the Flood.' Learned men, indeed, are of the opinion that the Tower of Babel was the metropolis of a universal monarchy. And, 'we of the Western World' (the phrase is pure Toynbee) 'have reason to believe ourselves of the posterity of Japheth'. This shrewd and able man seriously believed, with Filmer, that Charles I had possessed authority from Adam. But this authority had to be diminished for the smooth working of the State. Kings perceived that absolutism did not pay; that from poverty-stricken,

167

depressed subjects they could get nothing. 'Despair puts an end to Duty.' Seeing, therefore, that discretion pays, they diminished their rightful authority as the wise and businesslike thing to do. A characteristically English argument. It was by 'condescent' that they improved the condition of their subjects, a policy which made for contentment and prosperity. Such is Clarendon's reduction of the Theory of Divine Right to apparent good sense. After that there is, of course, no need for Hobbes' present of an illegitimate authority.

Here, he concludes, is the original and pedigree of government — quite different from 'that which the levelling fancy of some men would reduce their Soveraign to, upon an imagination that Princes have no authority or power but what was originally given them by the People'.[1] 'All power was by nature invested in one man (Adam), where still as much remains as he hath not parted with and shared with others to the good and mutual security of both.'

Now against this fine old tradition Hobbes' idea that 'an assembly of mankind can give absolute power to one man, unlimited by rules of justice and sobriety' looks the crude thing it is. Nor will he 'persuade men to change a government they have been under for centuries for an imaginary government by his rules of Arithmetic or Geometry, of which no nation hath ever yet had the experiment'. And what a state of affairs for trade would result from his exercise of a Hobbesian arbitrary power! There would be 'no liberty to buy or sell!' To 'contract with one another . . . to choose their own abode or their own diet' — then not considered a function of social

[1] p. 71.

justice. Clearly Hobbes' sovereign would be not much to depend on. As for his allegation that the study of classical authors makes for sedition — 'insurrections', says Clarendon, 'in these Western parts have come not from learned men, but from Jack Straw and Wat Tyler, who had never read Aristotle or Cicero'.

Hobbes had no right to accuse these classical writers or attempt to circumscribe the study of them. His own book is far worse. 'It would undermine monarchy more in two months than these great men have done since their death, and men would reasonably wish that the author of it had never been born in the English climate nor been taught to read and write.'

Mr. Hobbes should be more moderate. He should understand that 'It is a very hard matter for an architect in state and policy, who doth despise all precedents, and will not observe any rules of practice, to make such a model of government as will be in any degree pleasant to the governor or the governed, or secure for either.' Here Clarendon's criticism is again practically expressed. It seems difficult to answer.

Continuing on the theme of the impracticability of Hobbes' 'theorem of politics', Clarendon points out that Hobbes makes the worst of both worlds. For in spite of his advocating absolutism, he 'has to allow such a latitude in obedience to his subjects as shakes the very pillars of the State'. Consider, for example, his excuse to avoid fighting for his sovereign, whereby anyone can run away without committing treason. A Kingdom so divided, erected purely on a basis of calculating self-interest, cannot stand. On the contrary, a voluntary restraint of power on both sides for their mutual benefit is the best way of creating a successful society. Hobbes' method of putting the brake on an undiminished, unbridled power by allowing rebellion if the sovereign fails in his duty of protection, is a clumsy sophistry.

Convenient enough to usurpers, of course, but such an attitude is utterly subversive of real loyalty. Hobbes would 'make all Laws Cobwebs',[1] and no proper ruler would want his kind of sovereignty. Such government would have no prestige, for his laws are so arbitrary and crude, unhallowed by tradition, that no one would want to keep them. And, here, an interesting point, Clarendon comes near to Burke's feeling for the prestige of a traditional society. Clarendon can speak of an 'awful veneration' which a true commonwealth can inspire. Compare Burke, 'Our country is not a thing of mere physical locality: it consists in a great measure to the ancient order in which we are born.' So far back can be traced the roots of conservatism. Here already is a self-conscious tradition. The widespread assumption that Burke is the first to express it may have to be revised.

The crudity and repulsiveness of Hobbes' doctrine is further emphasized by his cynical perception of war as a cure for poverty, 'since it will provide for every man by victory or death'. 'They may', it implies, 'cut the throats of all men that are troublesome to them, which, without doubt, must be the natural and final period of all his Prescriptions in Policy and Government.' The internal nature of Hobbes' state is given away by the brutal advice which he has set down about foreign policy. Both can end only in chaos and bloodshed. Here, surely, Clarendon is right. In face of Hobbes' telling phrases, one is apt to

---

[1] p. 133.

feel that here is a master of realistic policy. Clarendon calls attention to the ugly cynicism which the cutting phrases mean. And political theory is concerned, not with a contest in rhetoric, but with the lives of men.

Working up to the conclusion of his critique of the second book of the *Leviathan*, Clarendon again roundly accuses Hobbes of having designed the book to conciliate the usurping government. 'Mr. Hobbes his *Leviathan* was printed and published in the highest time of Cromwell's wicked usurpation, for the vindication and perpetuation whereof it was contrived and designed.' It is to be hoped that the act of oblivion which protects the author will result in his doctrine 'expiring by neglect'.

Finally he sums up the conclusions of that doctrine.

First it implies that the sovereign's word is sufficient to take anything from any subject when there is need, and that the sovereign is judge of that need. This cuts across the principle of parliamentary control of expenditure — one of the fundamental advantages that the ruling oligarchy in the Civil War obtained and perpetuated by the settlement of 1660.

Secondly, the liberty of the subject becomes negative. The fundamental principle is denied that a man is assumed to be innocent until he be found guilty by process of law. Hobbes' liberty of subjects, says Clarendon, is 'only what in regulating their action, the sovereign later praetermitted'.

The third point is that nothing the sovereign can do is injustice. Its appalling consequences are sufficiently obvious. Moreover, the violation of natural law by killing innocent subjects is not merely an injury to them but to God. And the doctrine that no man has a liberty to resist the sovereign, but that criminals who have

171

already done so are justified in continuing resistance, is mere sophistry. And the whole edifice, as he has insisted before, is undermined if obligation ceases when protection fails.[1] Finally, Hobbes' doctrine implies an attack on property, for though property may be secured against one's neighbour, the sovereign can confiscate it. And, as for the right to transfer allegiance, it leads to treason. The danger envisaged by Bramhall 'that Mr. Hobbes takes his Sovereign for better but not for worse', is constantly present to Clarendon's practical mind. For both men knew from experience what government means. Thus, he concludes, though Hobbes' sovereign may appear to be on a pinnacle of power, he 'leaves him on such a Precipice from which the least blast of Invasion from a Neighbor, or from Rebellion by his Subjects, may throw him headlong to irrecoverable ruine'.

Hobbes' whole argument, he insists, is crude, unstatesmanlike and impracticable, apart from its blasphemy and pretentiousness. 'If these articles of Mr. Hobbes' creed be the product of right reason and the effects of Christian obligation, the Great Turk' (again) 'may be looked upon as the best philosopher and his subjects as the best Christians.'

With that, Clarendon, having dealt with the political implications of the *Leviathan*, proceeds to a detailed attack on Hobbes' Divinity. With this aspect of his argument we are not concerned. But he stresses its social effects; as the political doctrines attack the lawyers, the religious doctrines attack the clergy. And Hobbes puts the Bible on the same level as the Koran, by making its authority derive from the sanction of princes.

---

[1] Compare Bramhall, p. 124, and Whitehall, p. 176.

The book concludes with the observation, previously quoted, on Hobbes' lack of experience in public affairs. 'I should be very glad,' he says, 'that Mr. Hobbes might have a place in Parliament, and sit in Counsel, and be present in Courts of Justice, and other Tribunals, whereby it is probable he would find, that his solitary cogitations, how deep soever, and his too peremptory adhering to some Philosophical Notions, and even Rules of Geometry, had misled him in the investigation of Policy. . . .'

It is a criticism which none of the other adversaries of Hobbes could bring with the same weight of experience, and it is one which Clarendon might be expected to advance. For, as already emphasized, he came of just that class of country gentry, bred in the law; responsible if predatory; hard working, if insular, who were the backbone of the new bureaucracy, and whose administrative achievements are the most constructive aspect of the mid-seventeenth century in England. A man of good sense and integrity, seasoned in the ways of government, he has pointed out the practical implications of Hobbes' theory of the State.

CHAPTER IX

JOHN WHITEHALL'S INDICT-MENT OF HOBBES

THE last of Hobbes' critics to be considered was an able barrister, concerned to make political capital out of a denunciation of Hobbes. John Whitehall's *The Leviathan Found Out: or the Answer to Mr. Hobbes's Leviathan, In that which my Lord of Clarendon hath past over* appeared in 1679. It was the year in which the scare of the Popish Plot had roused the country to an extraordinary pitch of excitement, and when the threat of arbitrary rule, later attempted by James II, was already real.[1] Whitehall's contribution, as has been already emphasized, was topical, polemical and legal. An indictment of Hobbes with no quarter given, written with an eye to the political scene.

The book has the limitations, the verve and the brutality of its age and milieu. Its rancour is not academic, but legal and political. But because religion was still the driving force of political passion, Whitehall, who set himself to cover ground neglected or 'passed over' by Clarendon, devoted nearly half his attack to Hobbes' religious ideas. We are here mainly concerned with

---

[1] Whitehall's attack on Hobbes was published at the height of the political crisis following on the 'revelations' concerning the Popish Plot. Titus Oates's denunciations began in the autumn of 1678, and the judicial murders went on through '79 and '80. The year 1679 saw the dissolution of the Long Parliament of the Restoration, the imprisonment of Danby, the passing of the Second Reading of the Exclusion Bill and the dismissal of Shaftesbury. There were two general elections in that year, when the terms 'Whig' and 'Tory' first became current.

the first eighty-eight pages, with his able assertion of the
rule of law and with his defence of property — a theme
which Whitehall enlarged the following year into his
second and shorter attack on Hobbes, *Behemoth
Arraigned*.[1]

The theme of *The Leviathan Found Out* is stated in a
text from Job xli, 33, lifted by Whitehall from the
title page of the *Leviathan*. 'Upon Earth there is not his
Like.' After the obsequious dedicatory epistle to Heneage
Lord Finch, Baron Daventry,[2] of which some account
has already been given, Whitehall begins his polemic
with a reference to the custom of exposing 'monsters in
nature' for show. Hobbes' 'Monster in policy' deserves
a similar fate — particularly in 'Times of Danger and
Conspiracy'. That, for Whitehall, is the point. They
should be exposed 'for the Pleasure of the Wise and
Settled, and for the Benefit of those who are Unstable'.
In dangerous times we must 'keep within the bulwarks of
the law' — or else we shall be back in the plight of the year
1651, when, significantly enough, the *Leviathan* was
published, 'a time when our Nation groaned under the
Dissolution of all Ligaments of our ancient Government'.
Now, in view of a renewed menace (though the threat
came from a different quarter), he has 'undertaken Mr.
Hobbes in his *Leviathan*'.

Though his studies have 'bent another way' — to the

[1] *Behemoth Arraigned* contains little that is fresh to Whitehall's argument: it is a brisk
political pamphlet devoted to the defence of property. See above, p. 36.
[2] Heneage Finch, first Earl of Nottingham and Baron Daventry (1621-83), was the
son of Sir Heneage Finch, Recorder of London. He was educated at Westminster School
and Christ Church, Oxford. He was a lawyer and an administrator who took no sides in
the Civil War. In 1660 he became Solicitor General and in 1674 Lord Chancellor. He
was a constitutional lawyer and a Committee man, who attempted to assuage the political
passion roused over the exclusion controversy by compromise. In the year before his
death he was created Earl of Nottingham.

law rather than divinity or academic learning — and although Clarendon has answered Hobbes already, yet there is room, says Whitehall, for a lawyer to deal with those aspects of Hobbes which Clarendon, concerned with questions of Commonwealth of a transcendent nature, thought not worth answering. For in these times Mr. Hobbes has 'grown in reputation (why I know not) for parts and learning . . . so that many of his detestable errors and monstrous opinions have been embraced'.

Harking back again to the circumstance of the *Leviathan's* publication, he accuses Hobbes of political motives. He was 'bending his mind to the establishment of a new government, to be then erected, and the advance of himself in it, when our King was murthered and his royal son beaten from his rights'. Here is a glaring example of his poisonous doctrine that 'submission lasts only with power of protection', doubly dangerous today.

Lord Clarendon, he says, has fully exposed this personal aspect of the monster. He 'hath, I think, in all matters of this nature, made such a creature of Mr. Hobbes that I can think him capable of no other name than Leviathan'.[1]

This base personal manœuvre has affected Hobbes' whole edifice. 'Only let me observe what stuff this is, when searched to the bottom, to ground any government upon . . .' Subjects, he says, may desert their sovereign when he is in greatest need. This doctrine is 'sly and *Jesuitical* — likely to set the Prince against his people and the people against the prince, to the ruin of both'. Moreover, and here is Whitehall's second main point, Hobbes

[1] For Clarendon's argument on this point, see above, pp. 162, 167.

gives the property of the people to the prince, 'like a dear son of Sibthorpe and Manwaring'.[1] This attack on property can only make subjects weary of government, and endeavour to throw it off, 'that they may have something to be called their own'. It can only have consequences similar to the absolving of subjects from their allegiance, 'in case their Governour shall be imprisoned by a Popish Plot, or by any Invasion or Rebellion, though but for a Week, be made otherwise uncapable to exercise his Authority'. This, he says 'nick'd with Oliver Cromwel then and, the Papists now'.

The attack on Hobbes is again brought right into the arena of current politics.

Next, putting aside Hobbes' metaphysical arguments, 'which have been fully answered by a learned Bishop', and ignoring his attack on the Universities, and his opinions about witches, Whitehall concentrates on his own subject — on Hobbes' meddling with the law — 'which I could wish for sport-sake he had dipt a little more into . . .' First there is his fundamental denial, the denial of the law of nature. There is 'nothing good', he says, 'but as men account things so to themselves, or as they are made so by the person representing the Commonwealth or by an Umpire'. But, says Whitehall, the laws of nature precede man-made institutions.[2] He insists, with Lucy, that 'there is a such a thing as unnatural lust'; and what of the scriptural saying that a man sins if he 'commits adultery in his heart'? He must have offended a moral law. And if religion and morality have no sanction but fear and the ruler's command, the vilest 'Indian supersti-

[1] For these notorious Divines, see p. 96.
[2] Compare Locke's similar position. See J. W. GOUGH, op. cit., pp. 12-23.

tions' rank with civilized religion. But just as the scrip-
ture would have been valid without the Church, so
natural law is independent of institutions. And 'if it was
not justice the Heathen's Natural law was conversant
about, what was it'? Moreover, there is no difference in
the moral quality of actions, whatever their scale. If
government violates moral law, the wickedness of high
policy remains iniquitous. If this moral relativity be
admitted, one might argue that 'If a Russian ravish a
woman of great quality 'tis honourable.' Moreover, the
spiritual content is taken out of religion. Hence, perhaps,
Hobbes' anxiety to depreciate Christ's miracles — saying
that he only cured madmen, rather than cast out devils.
Anyway why did the herd of swine run down into the sea?
Mr. Hobbes may say 'they were mad swine to do so', but
there was much more in it than that. The devil was in
them as well. This was obvious to the Jews on the spot.
It is the supernatural element which counts. To deny
it is very serious: for by undermining the sanctions of
religion and natural law, Hobbes is trying to destroy the
foundations of society. Can it be he wants to make the
law 'odious and thereby open a gap for a standing army
...'? Here again is the note of political crisis. Why, the
denial of the foundations of law means that Cain's killing
Abel was lawful — all standards must go and property as
well. 'Oliver's army might, in the year 1651, take all the
property of the people of England, as they had taken the
King's . . . All subjects being absolved from their allegiance and there being no government in England but the
Army.' It is just the situation which will come about if
Hobbes' moral and legal principles are admitted. 'What
a good Trade a Captain of Horse of the same faith as Mr.

Hobbes might have had!... I wonder Oliver did not make Mr. Hobbes, for his healing Divinity, a Superintendent of Canterbury, with the power of a Troop of Horse to get as many inferior ecclesiastical lands into his hands ... by force, or that they did not give Mr. Hobbes a Patent under the Broad Seal of the Sword to cheat all he could for seven years.' With the current political tension in mind, Whitehall, throughout, puts Hobbes in the role of prophet for the arbitrary power of Oliver. Playing on those memories of the rule of the Sword and a standing army, he makes his denunciation of Hobbes a denunciation of the Catholic extremists of 1679.

But Whitehall is most concerned with Hobbes' misinterpretation of the law. For he denies the validity of custom, the basis of the English Common Law. Customs, says Hobbes, are not Laws 'by virtue of prescription of time, but by the constitution of their present sovereigns'. 'Here I suppose', says Whitehall, 'Mr. Hobbes principally aimed at supplanting our own Common Law.'[1] This argument, he says, again reflects the situation when the book was published, when it was 'most plausible to vest all in the army or him that should be turned up Trump'.

Yet the common law is the bulwark of liberty. 'For 'tis by the Common law that most men enjoy their estates, either real or personal. Now if length of time should not justify that property ... down goes the Common law and property with it. Then let the strongest take all, Witty Mr. Hobbes!'

Of course, there can only be one end to such nonsense.

[1] This point is also made by A. D. LINDSAY, op. cit., p. 15. Hobbes, he points out, was among the first political theorists to give statute law preference over common law, with all the consequencies leading to an Austinian concept of sovereignty.

Hobbes 'will destroy his country's law and make way for arbitrary power'.

Not content with this performance, Hobbes goes on to talk more nonsense about natural law. 'Having given the common law a Box on one ear to make it stagger, he hits it a clip on the other to get it upright again.' When, he says, an unwritten law is generally observed, and there can be no 'iniquity in the use of it', then it can be 'nothing but a law of nature, and obliges all mankind'. Now, legally speaking, this is arrant nonsense. You cannot equate custom with the law of nature, since customs vary. The law of nature is not man-made, but pre-existent. It is this denial and misunderstanding of natural law that makes Hobbes' argument legally disreputable.

Proceeding through the text of the *Leviathan*, looking for points passed over by Clarendon, Whitehall, like the Bishop of Derry, pitches on the doctrine that the prince can decide religion.

This, he says, is worse than the Turks. They will 'stick to Mahomet's doctrines in the Alcoran, let the Grand Seignor say what he will, but Mr. Hobbes is for changing it as often as the power of the sword shall command'. Here, again, Whitehall's argument is topical. If a Papist had been in command in 1651 'we ought to have embraced Romish idolatry. If a Jew had been general of the Army, and have bidden him [Mr. Hobbes] be circumcised, he would have done it. If a Turk had been turned up Trump and bidden Mr. Hobbes go to Mecca and worship at Mahomet's tomb, he would have done it; if a Persian had proved uppermost and have bidden him worship at Haly's shrine and say Haly was a greater prophet than Christ, he would have done it'.

Who but Hobbes would have argued thus? When Shadrach, Meshech and Abednego defied the temporal power of Nebuchadnezzar, and 'rather chose the furnace', God delivered them, 'in approbation of the doing'. Yet Nebuchadnezzar was a lawful sovereign. Or again, look at Daniel, delivered from the lions. Of course, says Whitehall, hammering home this personal indictment, Hobbes argued thus solely for his own interest. 'He thought he would secure himself in the year 1651, let the Turk, a Jew or the Devil wear the sword.' But it all comes back to his basic scepticism. 'Mr. Hobbes says that the existence or Being of things depends on Political Institutions, whereas Being of things ever was and ever will be absolute.' The last of these critics re-echoes the first, and the Restoration lawyer agrees with Filmer. It follows that a Civil Sovereign can 'model, but not alter the being of things'. And Whitehall refers the reader to Stillingfleet's *Origines Sacrae*.

Moreover, the consequences of Hobbes' impiety are fatal to missionary enterprise. He is worse than a Jesuit. 'Suppose a True Christian should go to Aurenge Zebe's Country.' His duty is to preach Christianity, 'that the heathen women amongst them might desist from burning themselves at the death of their husbands'. But Hobbes would conform, and countenance Suttee. And if temporal power should decide religion, 'this means that if a Papist get a Protestant into his power', the Protestant 'may without sin worship a wafer cake'. Further, if law is valid only when effective, then there is no harm in duels, 'because so few have suffered for the fact in late days'. Yet, 'they are contrary to the nature of a civilized state' — a topical point in Restoration London.

In his own field of the law, Whitehall again accuses Hobbes of gross and inept misinterpretation. If a subject deny his subjection, says Hobbes, he may be proceeded against as an enemy. Now this is nonsense. He can only be proceeded against under the law — the law of Treason. As a subject a man must be tried under law. Otherwise, arbitrary punishment would come in. 'But (God be blessed) there is no such thing as arbitrary punishment in England.' Here, on his own ground, Whitehall makes one of his best points. Again, Hobbes argues, it is sedition for any private man to judge of good and evil action. But this is pernicious doctrine, 'that private reason submit to publick'. A subject can only be convicted if he actually transgress the law — not for private opinions. Here, again, Whitehall is defending a fundamental liberty. If mere arbitary power is the basis of government, 'Ten highwaymen may take all they can get from any man because they are stronger, and any subject depose his King. (Good doctrine for a Popish Cabal.)' And 'When Sir Edmund Berry Godfrey was decoy'd into Somerset House and there strangled with a twisted Handkerchief by Romish Priests and Jesuits, there was irresistable power.' This highly topical allusion concludes the first half of Whitehall's book. The theological arguments make up the rest.

Hobbes and the Jesuits, says Whitehall, are after the same thing. When Hobbes 'falls on Cardinal Bellarmine and continues battering him for many pages together', it is hard to know which is the greater heretic. Bellarmine, the worshipper of false Gods, 'a wafer cake and pictures'; or Hobbes, 'the worshipper of no God at all, a stock or a stone when the sovereign commands, or when he shall change a Christian for an heathenish soil'. It is doubtful which of the two is worse. Again, Whitehall refers to Dr. Stillingfleet and 'to one of the sermons of the excellent Dr. Tillotson, another of our not only learned, but Protestant Divines'. Hobbes enervates the scriptures and his views on angels and the Pentateuch are unsound. He is a Manichee in blaspheming the goodness of God, who rules, according to him, not by love as the Creator, but simply by irresistible power. Moreover, Hobbes' materialistic idea of Hell is uncanonical. If, as he maintains, the wicked have bodies and can 'engender, eat and drink' the place must be in some respects enjoyable. Unless, of course, Hobbes was 'cruelly afraid of a luxurious wife', or else had been 'unneighbourly dealt with in his youth and afraid of the same hereafter'. After this rather Restoration point, and after much more theological argument, Whitehall emerges from the third book of the *Leviathan* to come to a vigorous conclusion.

Hobbes' supreme blasphemy, he insists, is his anthropocentric arrogance. 'This is to make man in Gods stead.' This arrogance makes him rail at Aristotle. 'Perchance hoping to make himself all the world over as great as Aristotle is in Oxford, and to bring in a new word of confusion, viz. Hobbes' *ipse dixit*. . . .'

Above all, he denies Aristotle's arguments for the rule of law. He says that Aristotle is wrong when he lays down that in a well-ordered Commonwealth 'not man should govern, but the laws'. To this Hobbes replies 'that words and paper affright nobody, but the hands and swords of men'. But here he only shows his misunderstanding of the law, which is above the actions of its agents. ''Tis true,' says Whitehall, 'the law is a Politic thing that can act nothing of itself without something that is natural conjoined to it, but, notwithstanding, 'tis properly called the Action of the Law, though the execution be by men's hands. Because it is the Authority of the law that empowers them, and through its efficacy they are justified in their actions.'

Here is the idea of government as a delegated, executive power, which runs through nearly all the writings of Hobbes' opponents. 'As a corporation,' says Whitehall, 'which . . . can really act nothing, yet notwithstanding the act of those they impower, is said to be their act.' So government respects the authority of the law.

Finally, he insists that Aristotle is right in depicting law as the bridle of arbitrary power, which is incalculable. 'And 'tis plain what Aristotle means, viz, that a well ordered Commonwealth is governed not by the uncertain will of the sovereign, but by laws established by the sovereign's power to make laws: in which consists, as my Lord of Clarendon hath shown, the greatest happiness of Prince and People.'

As for Hobbes, if he has misinterpreted the constitution out of ignorance, 'I am sorry for him, but if he said it to collogue with Oliver's army in 1651, and to persuade them into that arbitrariness which afterwards they exercised (and the Popish party have aimed at since), I will leave any Englishman to judge what he deserves from all lovers of their native country.'

It is a spirited indictment drawn up against Hobbes by this forceful and representative lawyer. He takes a few points and hammers them home: he does not go deep into metaphysical questions but he hits hard on his own practical level. He is thoroughly typical of his

184

class and age. Still probably representative of average opinion, too, in a curious twist he gives to his concluding argument. Hobbes, he says, wants to subvert not only the social but the cosmic order. He is actually 'positive for Copernicus'. He even says that time is determined by the earth's motion — 'and would have the earth itself turned upside down in nature'.

Hobbes, indeed, concludes Whitehall, reverting to his original text, is a law unto himself. 'And I will leave it to the judgment of any good and sober Man, whether Mr. Hobbes so far participates of the nature of the *Leviathan* as to have *not his like in all the Earth.*'

So the argument concludes, neatly, on the theme on which it began. Ordinary but cogent; a royalist, but an enemy to arbitrary power, Whitehall insists on the 'bulwarks of the law'. He invokes the memory of the arbitrary rule of Oliver, of his standing army. It is a warning of the danger from the Popish party in 1679. His book is at once a topical political pamphlet and a lawyer's indictment of Hobbes.

CHAPTER X

CONCLUSION

THE varied and eloquent contributions of nine critics of Hobbes have now been considered, and the ideas of Philip Hunton taken into account. How far, by modern standards, have these writers attained their objective? Have they vindicated a moral sanction to which government is responsible, and successfully defended the constitutional tradition Hobbes was attempting to undermine?

Their case may be conveniently examined under four heads. First, all agree that Natural Law confounds Hobbes' materialism. How far have they been able to maintain that venerable idea? Secondly, have they been able to confute Hobbes' cynical and deterministic view of human nature? Thirdly, have they been able to vindicate a constitution which embodies the distinction between government and society, and before which government can ultimately be called to account? For Hobbes, government created moral values: for his critics, as for Locke, it reflected them. For them it was useful because it was right, not right because it was useful.[1] In the fourth place, how far is Hobbes' theorem of government practicable? Or is he an original but wrong-headed genius; one who, as Bramhall said, 'never had a finger in mortar', and whose conclusions lead only to the enthronement of a dangerous and arbitrary power? These four considerations are worth taking in turn.

[1] See GOUGH, op. cit., p. 16.

CONCLUSION

By modern standards Hobbes' metaphysical assumptions seem hopelessly limited. It will be recalled that the basis of his political theory was a radical materialism. A crude behaviourist outlook, which regarded matter and motion alone as real. Mind, as Cudworth and More pointed out, he regarded as peripheral, 'nothing but local motion in the organic parts of men's body', and 'but a mere whiffling, evanid and fantastic thing.'[1] The Cartesian distinction between the I knowing and the thing known, which was to bedevil philosophy for so many generations, is here carried to extremity, the mind being regarded as a tabula rasa which passively reflects external phenomena, regarded, by a 'fallacy of misplaced concreteness', as somehow more 'real'. In Cudworth's phrase, 'Grave, solid and substantial senseless matter' is thought 'the most absolutely perfect of all things in the Universe.' Today, though the ideas of the Cambridge Platonists are out of fashion, opinion would incline rather to their side than to Hobbes. Mind, it is thought, puts into experience as much as it takes out, and cognition, an event in space-time, is creative in a sense which Hobbes would not admit. This modern rehabilitation of consciousness has superseded the mechanomorphism which formed the basis of Hobbes' scepticism. The brutal determinism of seventeenth-century physics, with its implication that the Universe is a vast machine, has given place to an acceptance of human consciousness as the climax of apprehended reality. Man appears no longer, as in Hobbes' view, a cog in a vast mechanism, but the artist through whose creative effort nature comes to full expression. This view, like Hobbes',

[1] See above, p. 42.

187

may be anthropocentric, but it is not materialist. Lord Russell, for example, a cautious authority, concluding his book on the *Analysis of Matter*, can write: 'I suggest that the world consists of steady events accompanied by rhythms, like a long note on a violin, while arpeggios are played on the piano — or of rhythms alone . . . As regards the world in general, both physical and mental, everything that we know of its intrinsic character is derived from the mental side, and almost everything we know of its causal laws is derived from the physical side. But from the standpoint of philosophy the distinction between physical and mental is unreal.'[1]

Hobbes' materialistic dualism gets short shrift here. His outlook on physics, with its concept of solid matter, gets no better treatment from Eddington whose views in this respect are still generally accepted. In his account of the structure of the atom, he wrote as follows: 'The atom is as porous as the solar system. If we eliminated all the unfilled space in a man's body and collected his protons and electrons into one mass, the man would be reduced to a speck just visible with a magnifying glass . . . Whatever further changes of view are in prospect, a reversion to the old substantial atoms is unthinkable.'[2] Later, Eddington concludes, 'Recognizing that the physical world is entirely abstract and without "actuality", apart from its linkage to consciousness, we restore consciousness to the fundamental position, instead of representing it as an inessential complication, occasionally found in the midst of organic nature in a late stage of evolutionary history.'[3]

[1] BERTRAND RUSSELL, *The Analysis of Matter*, p. 402.
[2] EDDINGTON, *The Nature of the Physical World*, chap. I, 'The Downfall of Classical Physics', pp. 1-2.
[3] EDDINGTON, op. cit., pp. 331-2.

Hobbes' mechanomorphism, if not his anthropocentric bias, today no longer commands assent.

Yet most modern philosophers would be disinclined to accept the cosmic order assumed by Hobbes' adversaries. For the attitude of all these critics is dogmatic. Whig political theory, like its ancestor medieval thought, depends on the belief in Providence. Although the outlook of these writers is predominantly rationalistic, for they believe that the truths of Christianity are self-evident to the light of reason operating within the sense data of immediate experience, it is fundamentally religious. A *mystique* — and in general a theocentric *mystique*. Society is the expression of the Will of a benevolent God. It has its own place in the cosmic order, and its own dignity. Hence Lawson's view that 'to think that the sole or principal Cause of the constitution of a civil State is the consent of men, or that it aims at no further end than peace and plenty, is too mean a conceit of so noble an effect'. Hence, also, Rosse's accusation that Hobbes is a Manichee, blaspheming life, since he regards himself as 'cut off from the first power of all powers'. Hence Bramhall's attack on Hobbes for his 'gross mistake of the Laws of Nature . . . A moral Heathen would blush for shame to see such a catalogue of the Laws of Nature'. Hence Hunton's assumption that it is 'no hard matter' to set out the 'end of Magistracie' . . . 'if we consider what was looked at when God ordeyned it. That was the Good of the society over which it was set'. Like the others, he believes in a benevolent Providence, and he regards sovereignty as an 'indivisible beam of divine perfection', since it reflects a cosmic order. Lawson insists that though power derives ultimately from the whole community, it is still bound by the laws of God, 'the only supreme Lord of life'. Eachard, characteristically, puts the matter in simple form. 'There be several things most firmly and undoubtedly good in themselves, and will continue to be so, let all the supremes in the world meet together to vote them down.' 'Very fine things,' replies Philautus, 'these goods and bads' . . . 'If the magistrate didn't make them, who did?' The two positions are irreconcilable. Clarendon's conviction that Hobbes' argument would undermine monarchy and make 'all Laws Cobwebs' and 'shake the pillars of the State', also derives from his feeling that society is something mysterious, sanctioned by God. Whitehall, again, sums up the position well. 'Mr. Hobbes says that the existence or Being of things depends on political institutions, whereas Being of things ever was and ever will be absolute.'

Here is a fundamental contrast, between the conservative outlook, later elaborated by Burke and Hegel, most vividly asserted by de Maistre in the early nineteenth century, and the positivist pragmatic approach. The perennial conflict recurs in different centuries and in different terms. There can be no compromise between this conservative affirmation or even between the belief that society is the expression of emergent will, and the 'mean conceit' that the state is a mere utilitarian conciliator of interests. On this first and fundamental point, whether society is the expression of a divinely sanctioned cosmic order, or the means of salvaging the wreckage of a Godless world, there can be no more rational decision than there could be in the seventeenth century. But in their vivid awareness of the questions at stake, these writers underline the profound and terrible implications of the problems raised by Hobbes. Again to quote Whitehall, 'this is to make man in God's stead'. It seems that Hobbes, like Nietzsche, regarded this operation as necessary.

Meanwhile, the critics all affirm the existence of some 'Natural Law', some mystical sanction for government. Their unanimity reflects a profound human need, emphasized by their indignation against Hobbes, by their awareness of danger. They all felt, with Rosse, that the denial of any sanction for Government other than power was 'a piece dangerous both to government and religion'. 'What stuff', says Whitehall, 'this is to ground any government upon . . . It is as full of damnable opinions as a toad is of poison.' Hobbes' state, in Clarendon's opinion, will not stand, since it will command no 'awful veneration'. For men, he says, are not rational, or alike, or equal. 'We have too much cause to believe that much the major part of mankind do not think at all.' Hobbes' attribution to them of a consistent and calculating self-interest shows him to be a poor psychologist, a man of the study, not of the world. The same unworldliness was often to be displayed by Hobbes' Utilitarian descendants in the early nineteenth century. Clarendon agrees with Filmer that Kingship must have absolute authority, modified in practice by 'condescent of grace'. Here, in an emotional loyalty, will be found the 'conciliation of interests' which Hobbes attempts to create by calculation.

This deeply felt need for an emotional sanction is reinforced by the appeal to conscience, of which Natural Law is held to be the reflection. The law of Nature is 'writ in men's hearts', says Lucy. 'In the breach of such law there is horror and dread, insomuch as a man cannot live. It is a prodigie to see a man without all Conscience.' It is the 'curb of conscience' says Rosse, that 'restrains men from rebellion'. For them this pre-existent Natural Law, seen by the light of nature, is obviously real, psychologically satisfying. Whether expressed in terms of Divine Right or metaphysical argument, they believed in it. Today it seems rigid and abstract: but it reflects the rationalization of primitive custom, inherited from Antiquity and the Middle Ages, and developed into loyalty to national institutions which commanded confidence.

We may conclude then, on the first point, that while Hobbes' dogmatic materialism is long outmoded (though most modern opinion accepts his anthropocentric outlook) the existence of the abstract sanctions he denied, or of the emergent values of neo-Hegelian thought, can neither be proved nor disproved. All that can be said is that they are a matter of faith, or of psychological projection, and that they appear necessary, in some form, as a sanction to government. The controversy thus remains undecided in its most fundamental aspect. On the other hand, the unanimity with which these critics insist on a mystical sanction for society, for Divine Right or Natural Law, for some embodiment of custom, or projection of conscience, is plainly something of which a pragmatic political science must take account. It indicates the weakness of Hobbes' attempt to devise a society based on cold calculation and unsupported by a myth. This weakness, apparent from the beginning, was to pursue all that stream of Utilitarian thought, even when it was freed from the taint of Hobbesian authoritarianism.

If we turn to the second count against Hobbes, his disparagement of human nature, it will be found closely connected with his metaphysical and religious scepticism. It provoked similar indignation. Far from feeling that Hobbes' anthropocentric and ruthless outlook emancipates the human race, these writers all feel that it belittles mankind. In the old view, humanity, in spite of original sin, had its place in a God-ordained hierarchy. The new scepticism struck cold upon them. They were appalled at this affront to human dignity. Rosse regards Hobbes as an obscene insect — 'shall the beetle thrust the eagle [Aristotle] out of his nest?' 'Men do not deal so maliciously for delectation.' The Hobbesian nature of man, says Bramhall, is a libel on human nature — 'worse than the nature of bears or wolves'. According to Hobbes, says Eachard, 'man is an arrant wolfe'. But this is contrary to experience. Mankind, he insists, is 'tolerably tame . . . methinks it is a great pity now at last to be sent to the Tower amongst the Lyons'; hence his long account of the 'Pineyards'.

Society, he argues, does not reflect such wickedness, or it would be paralysed by guilt and fear. If it were so, there would be no vitality or enterprise: 'men would huddle together like a brood of ducklings for mutual consolation, and get close into a corner with head under wing, and make not the least noise for fear of waking original sin'. Hobbes' pessimism outraged the confidence and vigour of late seventeenth-century England — a confidence natural in an expanding class and civilization to men of ordinary mind. Hobbes, like Machiavelli, probably concealed outraged sensibility beneath his indictment of the human race. But Clarendon is confident that 'God did not make men lower than the beasts'.

Like the first and fundamental point of disagreement, the second is not a matter of knowledge, but of faith and opinion varying according to environment. Hobbes' view was rather old fashioned against the predominant confidence of his age. He had more in common with the gloom of the later Middle Ages, or of the more conservative minds of Jacobean times.[1] By the later seventeenth century indeed, the prevalent climate of opinion was against his psychological egoism. In Cudworth's view, ethical truths are intuited by reason and are as unchangeable as the truths of mathematics. In More's opinion, the law of nature enjoins a rational benevolence. Locke's belief in the rationality of the mild brand of Christianity he professed contrasts with Hobbes' pessimism, and Locke's conclusions were more in harmony with the environment of his age. Similar views were later expanded in the eighteenth century by Shaftesbury, Bishop Butler, Frances Hutcheson and their followers. All agree that disinterested good will and sympathy are springs of action as natural as self love and reducible to it. Hobbes' Machiavellian view of human nature was to be swamped in the eighteenth century by an outlook which erred to the other extreme. There is the same confidence, too, in Seth Ward's defence of freedom of thought as in Locke's desire for religious toleration. Both are mildly optimistic: Seth Ward, in particular, aware of the greatness and the novelty of his age, regarded Hobbes as old-fashioned.

[1] See V. HARRIS, op. cit., pp. 8-42.

CONCLUSION

On the second point, then, it is plain that predominant opinion was on the way to assimilate the new, confident, but ultimately anthropocentric rationalism into traditional Anglican Christianity, and this optimism was typical of an expanding class and society. Hobbes, with, perhaps, deeper insight, saw the long-term implications of an anthropocentric world view and a deterministic psychology in the light of the apparently mechanical universe revealed by seventeenth-century physics.

III

There is a third question to be examined. How far have these writers vindicated constitutionalism against Hobbes? On this count, their case is clear and valuable. Here is a broad-based and able assertion of the traditional point of view, worth consideration today as well as in the seventeenth century.

All agree that government should be controlled by the superior authority of society, on the need for an alternative and ultimate standard.[1] As is well known, this view reflects an ancient pedigree, going back to Greek constitutionalism, that early rationalization of custom, and to medieval ideas of trusteeship. In the seventeenth century the emergent and creative concept of a general will, ascertainable by negotiation within a constitutional framework, was not yet defined. These writers, as already emphasized, are still based on the old concept of Natural Law, but it is adapted to a theory which reflects

---

[1] This distinction between government and society is well brought out by Mr. J. A. Thomas in his brief article on Hobbes' critics in *Economica*, 1926.

the institutions of the Protestant commonwealth in which they have their successful being. Lucy declares, like Burke, that institutions have their own sanctity: that men are born into a commonwealth, which is organic and not artificially contrived. He declares, with Cicero, that they are all 'citizens of the world', but the frame of government on which he insists is national. Here is an adaptation of medieval tradition to English society in the mid-seventeenth century. But that tradition is also rooted in classical ideas. Not only Rosse, the learned Jacobean divine, appeals to Aristotle, but Whitehall, the barrister of the time of the Popish Plot, who grounds his whole argument for the rule of Law on quotations from the Philosopher. And Aristotle is reinforced for Rosse by 'the chief learned of the Protestants', while Hunton appeals to 'the judgement of all the reformed Churches and Divines . . .' who have allowed resistance to their sovereign, 'Yea, our own famous princes, Elizabeth, James, Charles I . . . have justified the same.' Most notable is Lawson's attempt to pin down the sovereignty to society as opposed to government. 'Mens first loyalty is to be faithful to their Countrey.' He finds the 'supreme Power radical' in the 'fourty Counties'. He insists on the idea of a balanced commonwealth, citing Louis XI who 'removed all such as by right ought to have poysed him'. Like Rosse, who accused Hobbes of maintaining that 'tyrants and good princes are all one'; and of putting 'no difference between the father and the butcher of his country', Hunton makes the medieval distinction between a *princeps* and a *tyrannus*, quoting Fortescue and referring scornfully to German misinterpreters of the English constitution, to Arnisaeus and Besoldus. This insistence on the 'frame of govern-

ment', grounded in an ancient constitution, had been the
key to Hunton's argument. All power depends on the
consent of society, and although this power is dormant,
and although contract does not make monarchs 'mere
tenants at will', if a ruler violates his trust, and dissolves
'the frame of government and public liberty', the people
may transcend 'the frame of government they are bound
to'. Here is a position exactly anticipating that of Locke.
Hunton underlines this distinction between the original
act of the people constituting society, and their relation
with the form of government chosen, and he distinguishes
between societies which use their 'architectional power'
to opt for 'limited government' and those which chose an
absolute regime. Rosse, again, stresses the power of
choice. Hobbes' doctrine, he says, will 'hardly down with
a free borne people who choose to themselves princes,
not to tyrannise over them but to rule them'.

This clear cut concept of the original and inalienable
power inherent in society, as distinct from government,
is provoked by Hobbes' positivist justification of power in
its own right. Thus, although Clarendon repudiates the
triple division of powers advocated by Lawson and Hunton, both sides, Royalist and Puritan alike, assert that
society is not purely contractual and utilitarian. It is
sanctioned ultimately either by Divine right, moral and
absolute, as Filmer and Clarendon conceived it, or by the
whole commonwealth, a power, in Lawson's words, 'not
authoritative and civil, but moral, residing in reasonable
creatures'. Both sides are agreed, against Hobbes, that
the ultimate sanction must be moral and absolute, rather
than utilitarian and relativist. Hobbes' challenge provoked an uncompromising restatement of that position.

This obstinate maintenance of a standard by which government must be judged, is reinforced by a sturdy respect for the Law, the embodiment of constitutionalism. Hobbes, says Rosse, pretends that 'princes are not subject to their own laws'. Eachard complains that Hobbes presents princes with a greater power than they need. 'He gives him [the prince] such a full brimmer of Power . . . he hath raised him above our Form of Government.' Yet the King of England, bounded by the custom of the realm, 'thinks himself prince enough and is contented with his place'. But it is Whitehall who most ably expresses the limiting power of law. For Hobbes there are values intrinsically good 'but . . . as they are made so by the person representing the commonwealth'. He denies not only Natural Law but the validity of custom, enshrined in the English Common Law which he 'aimed at supplanting'. Hunton, following the same line, had insisted that institutions alone can bridle arbitrary power; he had appealed to history and to the growth of the Common Law out of custom, to the ancient polity of the Anglo-Saxons. Their government was 'limited . . . in the very *potestas* of it, of which sort the government of all the German nations was . . . They gave no tenure of conquest to their princes but kept their Laws'. Lawson develops this appeal to history, being convinced that the executive power was originally limited 'by certain rules which by antiquaries in Law . . . might be found out but are not'. The ancient constitution had been corrupted; it should be restored as a bulwark against arbitrary power.

Liberty, too, he insists, implies that a subject is free. So long as he keeps the law he is not only *liber* but *Dominus*. Whitehall carries on this tradition of limiting power by precise legal restraints. When Hobbes declares that if a subject denies his subjection he can be destroyed as an enemy, Whitehall insists that this circumvents the law of Treason and 'brings in arbitrary punishment . . . But (God be blest) there is no such thing as arbitrary punishment in England'. A man is innocent until proved guilty by process of law. Lawson and Whitehall are both emphatic that the power of rulers must be bounded by law, or they will 'little by little usurp it'. The bulwark of the law alone can prevent this outcome. Aristotle was right that no commonwealth ought to depend on 'uncertain will'.

The fear of arbitrary power unites all these critics. Hobbes embodied all their fears, dressed up in outlandish guise. All were provoked to assert the moral basis of society, its ultimate authority over and distinction from government. The two critics with the best legal grasp, like Hunton in his earlier and different context, had insisted with trenchant ability on the need for an ultimate sanction, embodied in the constitution and given precision by the Common Law. Here, provoked by Hobbes' powerful originality, is a formidable and valuable statement of the idea of constitutional commonwealth. It reflects the institutions, the interests and the beliefs of a representative cross-section of opinion in mid-seventeenth century England. While they do not approach Hobbes in originality, and seem sometimes even unaware of problems which his mordant genius raised, they make, as Maine was to do after them, a convincing case for the practical necessity of constitutionalism.

IV

The fourth count against Hobbes is almost unanimous. His theorem of politics, so arrogantly set out and recommended, is declared to be unstatesmanlike and impracticable. He is presented as a mere theorist, with no experience of politics and administration. On this count, Bramhall, Eachard, Clarendon and Whitehall — all men of the world — are emphatic. They spice their argument with mockery. Hobbes, says Bramhall, labours under a hopeless disadvantage: he has no idea of practical politics. For 'state policy', he declares, 'is wholly involved in matter and circumstances of time and place and persons, it is not at all like Arithmetic and Geometry'. Hobbes' theorem of government is artificial. Its consequences would 'put all to fire and flame'. Eachard, in particular, is concerned to point out the consequences of Hobbes' argument in homely and practical terms. He insists that, far from being a realist, Hobbes is led astray by his own eloquence; 'Philautus himself can smack his lips over an anchovy'. Clarendon takes the same line: 'under the show of explaining common terms he dazzles men's eyes'. Hobbes has the dogmatic arrogance of the theorist: he should remember that 'it is a very hard matter for an architect in state and policy, who doth despise all precedent, and will not observe any rules of practice, to make such a model of government as will be in any degree pleasant to the governor or the governed, or secure for either'.

Whitehall's whole argument turns on the outrageous impracticability of the Leviathan. It is like nothing on earth — in no relation to the realities of government —

the work either of a misguided or an interested theorist, either of a fool or a knave.

Nearly all the critics also hotly deny the reality and the use of Hobbes' state of nature, both as a fact and as an hypothesis. This common theme is most heavily stressed by Eachard and Clarendon, who deny, respectively, that humanity 'pricks up its ears and sets up its scut and falls presently to tearing and slicing and slashing', or that primitive man is obliged to 'worry and destroy all his own kind'. Whether the reality of this state of nature is seriously intended, or whether it is a figment of Hobbes' brain, 'of his solitary cogitations how deep soever', they nearly all insist that on this count his whole argument falls to the ground as unreal or misleading.

They are all emphatic that Hobbes' arbitrary power would be precarious and consequently inefficient. Filmer remarks that Hobbes' government would defeat its own ends; it would result in conflict and so defeat the purpose of nature, self-preservation. Rosse quotes Aristotle's saying that 'no commonwealth can be happy or continue long, but where the Prince is as well subject to the law as the people'. Above all, the doctrine that obligation ceases when protection fails was liable to set off violent political passions at the time. It receives strong condemnation. 'This is right dog's play', says Bramhall, '. . . it seemeth Mr. T. H. doth take his sovereign for better, but not for worse.' It is 'good doctrine for a Popish Cabal', says Whitehall. The book is a 'rebel's catechism', and although Hobbes' sovereign seems to be on a pinnacle of power, he is actually 'on a precipice'. Whitehall and Clarendon both insist on Hobbes' desire to ingratiate himself with Cromwell. As for his religious principles, they only make for hatred and confusion, or else for a tyranny worse than that of the Great Turk. And his ideas are also subversive of property, of the rights of inheritance fundamental to society. Hence, they insist, the danger of arbitrary power: it is not only wicked, it is inefficient. Such government, says Rosse, is mere slavery, 'which is the condition of those who live under the Turk, the Muscovite, Prester John, and the Magol'. It would have 'such power and authority', says Clarendon, 'as the Great Turk hath not yet appeared to affect'. It would not endure; for posterity, unbound by 'such an unthrifty condition of their parents', would call God's Lieutenant the 'Vizier Basha' and act accordingly. Such universal condemnation, reinforced by comparison with the most impressive Eastern absolutism current at that time, expresses the healthy belief these writers had in their own institutions, and their grasp of the supreme danger which confronts all societies — the abuse of power. Here they are in line with Locke, whose 'rationalization of accepted constitutional practice' has so much in common with their arguments, and whose covert hostility to Hobbes is apparent in his scornful and un-answerable phrase, 'this is to think that men are so foolish that they take care to avoid what mischief may be done them by polecats or foxes, but are content, nay think it safety, to be devoured by Lions'.[1]

For it was arbitrary power these writers feared. Put on their mettle by Hobbes' challenge, they state the consti-tutional and practical case against its dangers with sincerity, eloquence and truth.

[1] GOUGH, op. cit., p. 123.

CONCLUSION

V

On the first two counts against Hobbes, then, on his denial of a superior standard by which government can be judged, and on his maligning of human nature, his critics have asserted uncompromising beliefs. These affirmations, whatever their metaphysical validity, reflect a basic psychological need — the need for a mystical sanction for society, rooted ultimately in primitive custom, and for confidence in human instinct for mutual aid, essential for a healthy society. Their case, of its nature, cannot be proved. It remains a matter of faith and opinion.

On the second two counts, in particular on the need for a constitution, rationalizing the custom of a commonwealth and embodying the distinction between government and society, they have asserted a basic empirical principle of sound politics, one which is imperilled today not only by totalitarian dictatorships but by Parliamentary majorities, operating within a virtually single chamber legislature, and through a complex, centralized and increasingly independent bureaucracy. Finally their case that arbitrary power and intellectual tyranny make for inefficiency, but that government by consent within a framework of known standing laws makes for a more creative society, is backed by the evidence of history and current experience, and one still worth the widest support.

All these writers speak for a kind of constitutionalism. Even Filmer and Clarendon desire a moderated, legal, power. If Whitehall shows the most political rancour and uses his indictment of Hobbes to attack his opponents, he grounds his argument on an interpretation of the constitution, and upon Aristotle's insistence on the rule of Law. Clarendon, who shows the most statesmanlike grasp, is always practical in his approach and repudiates a raw and over-intellectualized utilitarianism. For him, as for Whitehall and Filmer, 'Being of things is absolute', but royal authority must be exercised with tact and common sense, or 'despair' will put an end to allegiance.

Eachard, refusing to be browbeaten by Hobbes' 'magisterial haughtiness', applies his wit and spirited common sense to something which he feels to be pretentious and, above all, unpractical. He writes, not to score a debating triumph, but to prevent Hobbes' doctrines corrupting the young. Bramhall, again, makes a practical approach: he is concerned with the consequences of Hobbes' ideas. Like Eachard, he possesses a command of striking phrase which makes his contribution outstanding for its power of invective among colleagues whose talents in that field are none of them negligible. Both Eachard and Bramhall have a saving sense of the ridiculous. It remains one of the most powerful weapons in the armoury of English and Anglo-American political thought. This hard-bitten, humorous common sense, owes much to Protestantism. It refuses to be overwhelmed by fine phrases, but asks what they mean and what they imply. It regards military adventurers with ridicule and distaste, and its fundamental decency is outraged by the antics of demagogues and dictators, for whose designs Hobbes and his followers were unwittingly to smooth the way.

In the minds of Philip Hunton and George Lawson, a rather different outlook is apparent. They are the most academically competent political theorists here considered. Hunton was not a direct critic, but by his grasp of the nature of sovereignty, by his idea of the triple division of powers, and by his precise and legalistic formulation of the principles of the constitution, by his admiration for old liberties, he greatly contributed to the Whig outlook which was to swamp the immediate influence of Hobbes and dominate the eighteenth century. It remained for the Utilitarian intellectuals to resurrect Hobbes in the nineteenth, and for writers of our own age to claim that he is the greatest English political philosopher, a claim which would have appeared fantastic to Locke or Burke.

Lawson, the ablest political theorist of them all, shared Hunton's feeling for historical precedent, for the old medieval tradition. His home-spun Nonconformist good sense reflects the atmosphere in which Locke formulated his ideas in the sixties and matured them through the following years. With Bishop Lucy, that bewildered but representative writer, who registered the protest of the conventional and the undistinguished, we have often some 'weak observations', but they are expressed in a pithy and eloquent style. He represents, in the Anglican way, a widespread school of thought; the view of ordinary kindliness and piety. And Seth Ward, with his defence of liberty of thought, his feeling that Hobbes is a grotesque anachronism, represents a new scientific outlook. It was to lead not to Hobbes' pessimistic materialism, but to the optimistic rationalism of the eighteenth century, though in the nineteenth it was to point to more searching conclusions.

Alexander Rosse, with his set-piece of Jacobean learning, his verbal fireworks, and his quaint cumulative erudition, was by no means a negligible writer on politics. There is much wisdom in his comprehensive argument; though his idiom belongs to an earlier age, he is one of the ablest of the critics. *Pareto legi*, he said, *Quisquis legem sanxerit*. Finally there is Filmer, the first critic, whose conviction of a moral and absolute sanction for society links up with the same feeling expressed by the last of them, John Whitehall. For though Whitehall, Clarendon and Eachard, with their clear prose, are a long way from Rosse and Filmer, they express fundamentally the same outlook. It is perhaps best summed up in the memorable phrase of George Lawson, 'for the English always desired to be governed as men, not as Asses . . . this is the quality of all understanding people of other nations'. Here is the motive common to them all. It is outraged common sense.

Original, far-ranging and politically wrong-headed, the *Leviathan* had provoked a representative vindication, in its contemporary idiom, of that method of self-government under law for want of which the world still staggers into successive crises and increasing peril. In their understanding of the dangers of arbitrary power, whether represented by the original genius of Hobbes or by its prophets and practitioners today, they are, indeed, in a good line of descent, one destined to expand from a local into a world influence. For it is the business of a constructive political theory to regard with caution the dogmas of systematizing philosophers, whatever their originality and eloquence, to reveal the appalling implications of the abuse of power, and to assert those proved principles of self-government which are the greatest contribution of our race to the history of mankind.

CONTEMPORARY BIBLIOGRAPHY

Besides the books examined in the text, the following
are among the works written against Hobbes in the second
half of the seventeenth century.

I

POLITICAL THEORY

Cocquius, G., *Vindiciae contra Tractatus T. Hobbessii*
(Utrecht, 1668)

Cumberland, R., *De Legibus Naturae disquisitio philo-
sophica* (1672)

Kortholt, C., *De Tribus Impostoribus Magnis* (Kiel, 1680).

Tyrrell, James, *A Brief Disquisition of the Law of Nature,
according to the principles and method laid down in the
Reverend Dr Cumberland's (now Lord Bishop of
Peterborough) latin Treatise on that subject. As also
his Confutations of Mr Hobbs's principles put into
another method*, with the right Reverend Author's
Approbation (1692)

II

THEOLOGICAL CRITICISMS

Dowel, John, *The Leviathan Heretical; or the charge ex-
hibited in Parliament against M. Hobbs, justified by the
refutation of a book of his, entituled the Historical
Narration of Heresie and the Punishment thereof* (Oxon.,
1683)

Pierce, the Rev. Thos (Dean of Sarum and President of
Magdalen College, Oxford), *Autokatacrisis . . . with
occasional Reflections on Master Hobbes . . .* (1658)
Tenison, the Rev. T. (later Archbishop of Canterbury),
*The Creed of Mr Hobbes Examined; in a feigned Con-
ference between him and a student of Divinity* (1670)

I I I

For Hobbes' views on the matter, see

Considerations upon the Reputation, Loyalty,

Manners and Religion,

of

Thomas Hobbes

of

Malmesbury,

written by himself

By way of a letter to a learned person

(Dr. Wallis, D.D.)

(1662)

See also:
Richard Blackbourne. *Vitae Hobbianae Auctarium* (1681)

For the best eighteenth century life of Hobbes:
The Moral and Political Works
of
T.H. of Malmesbury,
never before collected together
To which is prefaced,
the Author's life
(1750)

INDEX

INDEX

INDEX

Hobbes, Thomas—*cont.*
on human nature, 121; on resistance, 124; on sovereignty and
Natural Law, 128, 130-3; Eachard on, 138-54; 158, and Charles
II, 161; Clarendon on, 162; 173,
Whitehall's polemic against, 175;
184; a law unto himself, 185;
critics of reconsidered, 186; Cudworth and, 187; Lord Russell and,
188; and Eddington 188; 189, 190-5;
and Constitutionalism, 195ff; and
practical politics, 200-2; 204, 205,
206
Hooker, Richard, 14; and Lawson, 26,
41, 99
Hunton, Rev. Philip, 14; and Lawson,
26; Career of, 27; 28, 66; on Constitutionalism, 101-3; 166, 186,
189
Hurstbourne, Hants, birthplace of
William Lucy, 24, 27
Hutcheson, Francis, 194
Hyde family, connections of 158-9
(*See* Clarendon)

IRISH BISHOPRICS, revenues of augmented, 115
Isidore of Seville, St., 66

JAMES I, 107
James, II, 38, 122, 174
Jenkyns, Sir Leoline, 138n
Jews, dietary prohibitions of, 109;
Leviathan reserved for, 116; and
Gadarene miracle, 178; Hobbes
and, 180-1
John of Salisbury, 14, 66

KECKERMAN, BARTHOLOMEUS, of
Danzig, Calvinist theologian, 21, 69

LAUDER, WILLIAM, forgeries of, 18
Lawson, Rev. George, 14, 15; his
attack on Hobbes 25, 38, 46, 54,
66, 86; political views of, 86-100;

Lawson, Rev. George—*cont.*
Politica Sacra et Civilis of, 87; on
moral rearmament, 88; on divisions
of sovereign power, 93; 101, 112,
113, 143, 160, 164, 166, 189, 204;
on English method of government,
206
Leviathan (*See* Hobbes)
Lilburne, John, 41, 93
Lincoln College, Oxford, 115
Lindsay of Birker, Lord, 46, 49; on
Hobbes's state of nature, 58n;
179n
Lions in the Tower, 141; 164, 193,
202
Locke, John, 14; 25; and Hunton, 27;
28, 41; and Hobbes, 47; 86, compared with Lawson, 98; 108, 112,
131, 186, 194
Lombard, Peter, irrelevant to seventeenth century Universities, 74
Louis XI, cited by Lawson, 95; 196
Lovelace Papers, 14
Lucy, Francis, 24; Rosse's dedication
to, 62
Lucy, William, Bishop of St. Davids,
his attack on Hobbes origins, and
career, 23-5; 38, 54, 72; his case
against Hobbes, 75-85; assertions
of 86; 91, 101, 102, 143, 164, 177,
191; and Burke, 196; 205

MACLEAN, A. H., on Lawson, 25n,
100
Machiavelli, 193, 194
Magdalen College, Oxford, Clarendon
at, 23, 159
Magdalen Hall, 74, 159
Magna Charta invoked, 111
Maine, Sir Henry, on Hobbes, 56; 133,
199
Malmesbury, birthplace of Hobbes,
53, 159
Manichees, 63; Hobbes compared to,
64, 70, 183

213

INDEX

Manwering, Roger, Bishop of St. David's, on taxation, 96; 177

Martin, Edward, Dean of Ely, 96

Masenius, 18n

Mathew, Tobias, Archbishop of York 28, 114

Marx, and Hobbes, 44; 159

Melanchthon, 21, 69

Mersenne, 53

Milton, John, and Lauder, 18, 57; decentralizing projects of, 94

More, Shropshire, Lawson Rector of, 25, 187

More, Rev. Henry, on Hobbes, 42-3, 194

Nebuchadnezzar, metamorphosis of, 19, 181

Netly, 76

Neville, Henry, author of the *Isle of Pines*, 142n

Noah, 19, 66

Oakeshott, Prof., on Hobbes, 43; 47

Paracelsus, 148

Penruddocke, Colonel John, and Hyde family, 158

Persians, Laws of, 120, 180

Peter Martyr, on Aristotle, 69

Pierce, Thomas, Dean of Salisbury, 23

Pike, William, 24, 25. (*See* Lucy, William)

Pines, Isle of, 141, 142n

Plamenatz, J. P., on Hobbes, 43; compares Bentham with Hobbes, 59n

Popish Plot, occasion of Whithall's pamphlet, 37

Powell, Anthony, 55n

Quakers, regarded as dangerous, 143

Raleigh, Sir Walter, his History criticized by Rosse, 18, 19, 61

Ramsey, Andrew, his poem on the Creation, 18n

Richelieu, Cardinal, Political Testament of, 130n

Romans, on the laws of war, 122

Rosse, Rev. Alexander, of Southampton, 14; Scottish origins and successful career of, 17; his Works, 18, 19; 54; Criticism of Hobbes, 61-71; poem to, 62n; 75, 189, 191, 192, 193; and Whitehall, 196n on freedom 197; 205-6

Russell, Lord, his 'Analysis of Matter' quoted, 188

St. Paul, on human nature, 90

Salisbury Cathedral, 23; City, 158

Savernake, Forest, 76

Scaliger, 21, 69

Shaftesbury, Lord, 194

Sheldon, Archbishop, patron of Eachard, 138; 147

Sibthorpe, Rev. Robert, Royalist Divine, preaches Passive Obedience, 96, 177

Sidney Sussex College, Cambridge, Seth Ward a Fellow of, 22; Bramhall educated at, 28; Cromwell at,28

Socinianism, Hobbes accused of, 64

Somerset, Duke of (*See* Hertford, Marquis of)

Southampton, Free School at, 17, 18

Stalin, compared with Grand Turk, 144n

Stuart, Lady Arabella, and Lord Hertford, 76

Stubbs, Bishop, his views anticipated by Hunton, 110

Swift, unjust to Eachard, 138n

Tacitus, favourably compared with seventeenth-century historians, 94 cited by Hunton on primitive Germans, 110

INDEX

Thomas Aquinas, St., 65

Thomas, J. A., 195n

Thucydides, 47, 94, 152

Thynne, Sir John of Longleat, 158

Tincleton, Dorset, 159

Tottenham House, 76

Trinity College, Oxford, and Seth Ward; Lucy educated at, 24

Turks, Government under, 67, 68; fear of Grand, 144, 166, 172, 180, 202

UTILITARIANS, 7, 43, 191, 205

Ussher, Archbishop, 116n

VESEY, Bishop, his views on Hobbes, 29, 116, 117

WADHAM COLLEGE, Oxford, Seth Ward Fellow of, 22; Hunton at 27; advanced thought in, 74

Wallis, Dr. J., his controversy with Hobbes, 22; 54, 154

Ward, Dr. Seth, Bishop of Salisbury, 21-3; 54, his views against Hobbes, 72-5; 114, 165, 194

Webster, John, puritan and divine, and Seth Ward, 22

Wentworth, Sir Thomas, afterwards Earl of Strafford, Bramhall, chaplain to, 28; 49, 121

Westbury, Hunton Vicar of, 27

Whitehall, John, Barrister, 15, 35-8, 66, 86, 163, 174-85, 190, 191; and Rosse, 196; vindicates common law, 198; 199, 200, 203, 206

Willey, Prof. Basil, quotes Cudworth on Hobbes, 42n; 48n; on Hobbes's metaphysical views 50; 121

Wilkins, Dr. John, Warden of Wadham, 22

Wood, Anthony, on Lucy's 'Observations', 25; 115n; on Eachard, 138n

XENOPHON, 94

YOUNG, JOAN, of Durnford, Wilts, 158

ZANCHIUS, HIEROME, of Strasbourg and Hiedelberg, 21n, 69